A Collective Breath

A Collective Breath

Stories of Being Black in America and Visions of Change

COMPILED BY BRIDGETT McGOWEN-HAWKINS

BMc
TALKS

Published by BMcTALKS Press, a division of BMcTALKS, LLC, Chandler, Arizona.

Disclaimer: This book is for educational purposes only. The views expressed are those of each contributor and should not be taken as expert instruction or commands. The reader is responsible for his or her own actions. Adherence to all applicable laws and regulations, including international, federal, state, and local governing professional licensing, business practices, advertising, and all other aspects of doing business in the United States, Canada, or any other jurisdiction is the sole responsibility of the purchaser or reader. Neither the author nor the publisher assumes any responsibility or liability whatsoever on the behalf of the purchaser or reader of these materials.

Unless otherwise specified, the views expressed in this publication are the responsibility of each contributor and do not necessarily reflect or represent the views of BMcTALKS Press, its owner, or its contractors.

Volume pricing is available to bulk orders placed by corporations, associations, and others. For details, please contact BMcTALKS Press at info@bmtpress.com

The publisher greatly acknowledges all who contributed to this book.

FIRST EDITION, THIRD PRINTING

Library of Congress Control Number: 9781953315007

ISBN: 978-1-953315-00-7 (hardcover)
ISBN: 978-1-953315-01-4 (eBook)

Printed in the United States of America.

To Parker

This book is also dedicated to every person who recognizes, understands, and celebrates the strength and the stories of black Americans and to everyone who has a vision of change.

Contents

Introduction

In early June of 2020, many of us found ourselves unable to sleep…unable to function normally…unable to comprehend that, once again, a Black man found himself unable to breathe and ultimately met his demise at the hands of police.

You may have also found yourself wanting to do something. We at BMcTALKS Press certainly found ourselves in that position.

By adding this book to your library, you show that you have decided you want to be part of a positive impact in light of what we know is yet another sad page in our nation's history and another undeserving occasion for the Black community with the murder of George Floyd. Thank you for seeking an avenue to add to or learn from the conversation, to ensure you do not sit silent, to ensure you do something. But do not keep the knowledge to yourself. Share what you learn herein with someone you know would *never* pick up a copy of this book and read it.

The contributors to *A Collective Breath* include a wide variety of well-educated Blacks who are civic leaders, entrepreneurs, business owners, and professionals who are involved with their families, communities, and religious organizations. Their candid, personal thoughts and feelings reveal the many challenges that we face in America today, but they also offer ideas for solutions and actions to pave the way to a brighter future. Specifically, contributors tell of what it is like to be Black in America. Some address their reactions to the George Floyd murder and the many instances of racial injustice they have seen in recent years and decades.

Others give their reactions to Breonna Taylor; Ahmaud Arbery; or other Black men, women, and children whose deaths are connected to questionable acts of injustice at the hands of police or others. Some recount personal experiences with law enforcement or others in society that further raise their awareness of their Blackness. And everyone was encouraged to not hold back and to pour into their writings. We want you to see what we see, hear what we hear, and feel what we feel.

And we feel a strong need to move others to fully understand the purpose behind the Black Lives Matter movement. In the aftermath of the Boston marathon bombing that killed three people and injured hundreds of others on April 15, 2013, "Boston Strong" was not met with "all cities are strong." When a gunman, who killed himself on October 1, 2017, injured more than 800 and was responsible for the deaths of fifty-eight people that night plus two others who died in 2019 and 2020 from the injuries he inflicted on them while they innocently attended at a country music festival, the "Stand with Las Vegas" slogan came to be and nobody exclaimed in response to it or with the intent of being more inclusive "Who's standing with my city when people get shot here?" "Black Lives Matter" should not be met with "all lives matter." Yes, all lives *do* matter. At the same time, as Americans, when there is a crisis in a group, we have always rallied around that group and shown our support. The rally is not meant to discount any other group but is meant to bring awareness and support to the group that is currently hurting.

A Collective Breath is not a book meant to bash law enforcement, the justice system, or the police. This IS a book meant to shed light on how some of us feel as Black people in America and what we believe must change for the sake of the forthcoming history of our race and our country. It is a book where we take a collective breath— the breaths that George Floyd, Manuel Ellis, Javier Ambler, Eric Garner, Daniel Prude, and so many others could not take—to document for the world how we feel in this moment and what believe needs to change today so our tomorrow leads us all a step closer to a reality and existence of which everyone can be proud.

A Letter to the Reader

AARON L. HAWKINS and BRIDGETT McGOWEN-HAWKINS

Hurt people find ways to hurt people.

In August of 1619, the Dutch ship *The White Lion* landed at the port in Jamestown, Virginia, loaded with more than twenty Africans. In exchange for food and money, the Africans were offered to the colonists as indentured servants, setting in motion a life for Blacks in a new country that would have us, more than 400 years later, questioning the value others place on our life in America and that would have us questioning what kind of internal pain could have been inflicted upon a people that compels them to treat others with such indignity and disgrace.

How dare a people act with such cruelty and self-ascribed superiority, ripping humans from their own land and the only existence they knew up to that point; sail them across an ocean on an unimaginable voyage fraught with strife, fear, and confusion to a strange land; and offer them up as chattel to another group of strangers? What right does anyone have to do that? Moreover, how are the aggrieved supposed to accept this act and the unrelenting systematic inhumane treatment that comes with not being seen nor being treated as equal human beings among those who may not look like them but who bleed the same, who hurt the same, and who love the same? How are the aggrieved supposed to respond? What are the aggrieved supposed to do? And what are the aggrieved supposed to think?

Given the history of our arrival in this country and with statistics from the first two decades of the twenty-first century uncovering the disproportionate rate at which Blacks are killed by police, one cannot help but wonder to what extent our lives matter to those who repeatedly, carelessly, and senselessly end those lives.

By the summer of 2020, with the news of one death after another death after another death of Blacks in America, we questioned what happened and how in the world we got here.

Did the color of the victims' skin play a factor in their deaths? Are the media overreporting these stories, creating a problem where there is none and under-reporting or not reporting at all the news of White communities that are privately reeling from repeated and senseless attacks on their people? Are we imagining all of this?

As we see, hear, and read the stories, we are reminded of our own personal encount-ers with the law, with instances of intentional and unintentional or blatant and hidden racism, or moments of microaggression, adding fuel to the flames of sadness and frustration. Is our perception of how others value (or devalue) the life of a Black person in America being driven more by statistics or by stories?

In 2015, *The Washington Post* began compiling data from news outlets, social media, and police reports to get an accounting, from around the country, of the number of fatal shootings by on-duty police officers.

What *The Washington Post* learned was that more White Americans are killed that Black Americans are shot by police at a *disproportionately higher* rate.

In his July 16, 2016 article, "Aren't More White People Than Black People Killed by Police? Yes, but No," Wesley Lowery of *The Washington Post* writes "According to the most recent census data, there are nearly 160 million more white people in America than there are black people. White people make up roughly 62 percent of the U.S. population but only about 49 percent of those who are killed by police officers. African Americans, however, account for 24 percent of those fatally shot and killed by the police despite being just 13 percent of the U.S. population. … [T]hat means black Americans are 2.5 times as likely as white Americans to be shot and killed by police officers."

Lowery goes on to add that "U.S. police officers have shot and killed the exact same number of unarmed white people as they have unarmed black people: 50 each. But because the white population is approximately five times larger than the black population, that means unarmed black Americans were five times as likely as un-armed white Americans to be shot and killed by a police officer."

Does race have anything to do with the disproportionate number of killings? The data suggest it does.

However, where we have utmost clarity is that we, along with the rest of the world, watched in horror over and over again as the video played of a White police officer holding his knee to a Black man's neck for nearly nine minutes on the pavement of a Minneapolis street in May of 2020.

What we do know is bystanders pleaded, to no avail, for the officer to get off him.

What we do know is that knee ended up killing him.

What we do know is that Black man was George Floyd.

And what we do know is he wouldn't be the last one to suffer his death at the hands of police and have it captured on video in the United States.

For us, a Black man and a Black woman in America, it sparked conversation after conversation at the dinner table.

We were reminded of the times we've been "mistaken for" and/or called the name of another Black person because, instead of attempting to make distinctions among us by looking at our individual skin tone and unique facial features, which are the characteristics that most notably set Blacks apart from each other, those from non-ethnic backgrounds may regularly and, in the case of Blacks, ineffectively and erroneously use hair color and eye color as a means for distinguishing one person from another. In short, when you make yourself better aware of how to truly identify what makes each of us unique, we really do not all look alike.

We were reminded that we have to have different conversations with Black children about how to behave if they ever encounter the police—likely conversations that are vastly different from the kinds of conversations parents of non-Black children have, if they have these kinds of conversations at all.

A person should not have to think like us or act like us or sound like us or look like us for that person to matter to us.

In June of 2020, we experienced a bolder reminder of the reality of our existence in America, and we asked questions.

What is happening?

Why is it happening?

What can we do?

How can we find a way to make a difference?

We decided to write.

We decided to ensure that we did not remain silent, that we did not put ourselves in a position to look back on this chapter in history and find ourselves unable to say we did something. And we decided to ask others to join us and take a collective breath and tell our stories of what it's like to be Black in America and the change we believe needs to come.

We recognize our experiences are not unique to us. On the following pages are accounts we recall from our time living in Texas and Arizona that have us, as Black people, questioning whether our race fueled what happened and what was said. On one hand, can our race have absolutely nothing to do with any of these occurrences? It's possible.   On the other hand, do we have to question whether it plays a factor? Most certainly.

We also recognize that each experience detailed by everyone in this book, when viewed in isolation, may not be seen as cause for concern or alarm. But to the reader, especially the non-Black reader, who draws this initial conclusion, please be cognizant of the fact that we wake up every day knowing—as unfortunate as it is— that any one of these experiences—any slight, indignity, or injustice—can (and likely will) happen again and again and again on any given day of our Black lives.

I Am More Than What You Think I Am
Aaron describes what it's like to feel invisible.

When I was growing up and attending school in a predominantly Black school district, parents and teachers alike told us we had to be twice as good and work twice as hard as our White classmates.

Teachers would always teach the same things mom and dad would teach: Making a "B" is not enough. And I was conflicted because I was happy with a "B"! But the message was clear: if you want to get out and compete, then you have to know more than just enough.

Once I arrived to high school, that's when things changed. Specifically, when I started playing sports, coaches catered to us, so being told to do our best and to go beyond the minimum in the classroom, as I'd been taught in elementary, went by the wayside. However, coaches encouraged you to do your best on the field.

It felt as if coaches gave Blacks a lot of leeway because they wanted those students in particular to compete in sports, but after the season was done, the sentiment from the coaches was essentially "Run along, little kid. I have no more use for you." At the time, it made me feel strange, but I did not give it much attention. However, in hindsight, it made me not want to play for someone who did not have any interest in speaking to me after the season. I did not fully recognize and process this feeling at the time because I was usually finishing one season and moving on to another sport, or I would go home and get over it quickly thanks to encouragement from my mom and dad, who would tell me to move along and not worry about it.

I specifically recall having an English teacher who was also a coach. He assigned a five-paragraph paper, and I received a D on it because, in part, my conclusion paragraph was missing. Upon receiving my graded paper and feedback, I asked the teacher to help me with understanding how to write an effective conclusion paragraph, and his response was to not worry about it: "You passed."

There was no interest in helping me be better. Here I was, a student-athlete coming to him for help, wanting to improve, wanting to learn, but the minimum requirement had been met; I had done well enough to earn a passing grade, so it seemed the teacher didn't value me enough to develop the student side of my student-athlete status. As long as my grade was good enough to play sports, that's all that mattered.

Invisible.

The same went for Spanish class. As long as I was playing sports, the Spanish teacher, who was not a coach, would pass me, but when I wasn't playing sports, he wouldn't pass me.

Those were not isolated incidents, resulting in me arriving at college and having to relearn how to fully develop a written body of work, because for years, I wrote just well enough to pass. It became clear to me early on that I had to turn things around, and fast.

In high school, unless I was dribbling a ball or running for the end zone, I felt invisible.

Even today, as a college graduate and a fully grown man, married and with a child, while wearing my uniform at work, I am made to feel invisible at times.

As a light rail supervisor in a major US city, working the second shift, I see all kinds of events: falls, assaults, car accidents, hit-and-runs, domestic violence, stabbings, shootings…you name it.

There have been instances where I was the one who put in the call for police or fire to come to a scene, and when the official arrived, he would walk right by me and instead approach my White coworker, resulting in the co-worker having to send the police or fire official back to me.

It makes me feel that the White guy is more important to talk to than me.

The first time it happened, I said something. "Hey, man. Why did you pass me up? You walked right by me, went to him, and now you have to come back to me."

To be honest, I'm not sure which upsets me more—the feeling that the White coworker is considered to be more important than me or the fact the official wasted valuable time going to the other end of the platform, then having to return to where I was.

I go on to add, "I'm the scene commander. You have to talk to me."
The response is usually some BS answer—"Oh. I didn't know you were the one who called in."

Really? Okay.

I give them the benefit of the doubt because they don't know what they're walking into when they arrive on the scene of a call. But at least give *me* the benefit of the doubt and ask me instead of walking past me.

Don't walk by me as if I'm invisible.

This invisible feeling often compels me to use everything in my skill set to prove "I am here." It feels like you have to figuratively flex your muscles and pull out your college transcript or your résumé to get any recognition for what you're doing.

At work, I can fly under the radar, mind my business, perform the duties of my position as expected, and no one knows what I'm doing. But when I start sending emails, writing up employees for not adhering to a rule or policy, or sending in reports, I get responses from new members of management such as "I didn't know you could do all of that!" My thinking is What do you think I'm a supervisor for?

I'm more than the train-troubleshooting, basketball-playing guy from Texas that you think I am.

Not Another Mad Black Woman

Bridgett describes feeling invisible and remaining silent to avoid getting unfairly labeled.

While I was in the employ of an edtech company and leading a workshop in the Denver area around 2012, the workshop venue contact walked right past me; went directly to my manager, a White woman; and started talking to her as if she was the contact for the event. She let him finish his question, then immediately pointed in my direction, put the biggest smile on her face, and said, "Today, I work for her."

To write "I felt like a rock star in that moment" would be a gross understatement. My manager had SO MUCH respect for me—not just on that day and not just Monday through Friday, but on ALL days of the week. She never hesitated to speak up for me and advocate for me, no matter what. I am sure her magnanimity partially came naturally, and it partially came from having a manager of her own who, too, would go to bat for anyone on our team.

But back to Denver. What struck me in that moment was the fact the event venue employee simply returned to where I was standing and matter-of-factly commenced with addressing me with his query. A little bit of heat crept up my neck and to my face. (That happens a lot when I get annoyed.)

It took everything in me not to ask him why he made his assumption. It took everything in me not to ask him if he was aware of what he just did. It took everything in me to refrain from saying anything. Because if I had, then I would have run the risk of getting labeled as another mad Black woman. I was ever so aware of needing to remain cool and calm to ensure I did not have him (and possibly my manager) thinking I had made something out of nothing.

I was aware because, after once voicing my opinion in a no-nonsense manner to a coworker, I was labeled as being angry when that could not have been further from the truth. To write that's maddening is an understatement. The bottom line was I was done with the conversation. I stated my opinion, and it was a wrap. She saw the abruptness as madness; I saw it as "We've been working all day at this conference venue, and I'm done with this discussion. I'm tired; I don't feel like code-switching anymore; and frankly, I'm ready to put up my feet and sip a margarita." When a Black person speaks with conviction, passion, authority, assertiveness, assuredness, certainty, or even sternness, please stop thinking it is anger because…well…it's not anger. It is not. It is simply how some of us express ourselves. But out of wanting to not be misunderstood or misperceived, we may oftentimes keep our comments to ourselves, opting to listen twice as much as we speak.

On a regular basis, I am cognizant that I represent not only myself but ostensibly every Black woman. I am cognizant of the possibility that when someone has an encounter with me, that that person may paint with a broad brush, thus overgeneralizing, and surmise that is the kind of experience to expect from *all* Black women. I endeavor to be mindful of my behavior and reactions. I am not always successful, but as often as possible, I endeavor.

It did not dawn on him what he had done or how it may have made me feel, or it may have dawned on him and he did not care. He had no visible signs of embarrassment, nor did he express any apology for assuming that out of the two of us, both of whom were professionally dressed, it had to have been the White woman and not I, a younger Black woman, who was the one running the show.

What also struck me was the grace and kindness with which my manager handled the situation. Her clever and swift act coupled with those simple five words, "Today, I work for her," gave me a boost of power and confidence that was indescribable. It was a moment I have always cherished and one I will never forget.

At the same time, I will never forget how it felt to not be seen, to be regarded as being invisible…in that moment, I was slapped in the face with this stark and sad reality: for that man and, quite likely, for countless others, when given a choice to assign authority to either a Black person or a White person, it is the White person who will most likely receive an instant designation as the one who's steering the ship.

Does My Blackness Diminish My Authority?
Aaron describes an experience that made him feel dismissed while on the job.

One rainy evening, a man was at the platform at Third and Jefferson with his back to the train. He was on the rumble strips, so I said, "Will you step out the way so the train can come through?"

"Who are you talking to?"

"You."

"Oh, the train ain't gonna hit me."

"No, it may not, but it's not going to pass you until you get off the rumble strips."

He continued to stand where he was, not making a move.

But when I signaled for the train to stop, his attitude changed. It was then that he realized I was a member of metro personnel.

Clearly taken aback, he said, "I wasn't used to you being here. I'm used to Bob Fleming being here."

"Well, Bob's not here. I'm here today."

Am I being fair? With the rain jacket covering my uniform and no company insignia on it or my hat, did that put me in a position to get dismissed?
Or is it because I am Black that I was dismissed, and my authority was diminished?

I Am Not an Employee. I Am a Patron. And I Am Here.
Bridgett describes being seen and not seen.

How many times have I been mistaken for a flight attendant or a sales associate in a department store? I cannot count. Granted, the dark-color skirt suits and navy, gray, or black dresses I often wear when traveling on business do not help. In all honesty, this may be an indirect compliment to me because people who mistake me for a member of the flight crew usually quickly apologize and follow up with "Oh?! You just seem like you really know what you're doing, so I instantly thought you were an attendant."

Could it be the air of confidence I have; the frequency with which I travel that makes all-things-travel second nature to me; or my ever-present goal to never look like a victim, especially when I'm far away from home?

Or is it because I am Black that this happens? I do not know.

I am, however, less confused as to why I am mistaken for a sales associate in a department store, and I more firmly believe the color of my skin is at play. Although I have my handbag on my shoulder or on my arm—just like the non-Black person who approached me—and although I have on no name tag—just like the non-Black person who approached me—I still have received questions from patrons about whether a particular wine glass is in stock or if I can go in the back and bring out a pump in a size seven. (And as an aside, a tan shoe is a tan shoe; its color is not "flesh

12

tone." The same goes for bandages and hosiery. Everybody's skin tone is not that so-called flesh-tone color. When labeling items' color as such, the unspoken assumption is a person's skin tone that matches that color is the standard. Not everyone's skin tone resembles a shade of tan or beige.)

Why assume that I am not also shopping? Why assume I must be working? I'm a patron—just like you.

Then, on the opposite end of the spectrum, there are instances when I am *not* seen while out shopping, especially when I patronize more affluent areas. More often than not, I witness certain White women in these areas who have an affect and an air of personally perceived superiority combined with a refusal to acknowledge that another human, specifically that a Black human, is in their midst when passing me on a sidewalk or when crossing my path in a store. However, I am here.

Let me be very clear: I LOVE self-confidence. (Anyone who's seen me at a microphone knows I eat, sleep, breathe, and believe in some self-confidence!) However, when one exudes an air of self-confidence that is tinged with an intent to make others feel subordinate, therein lies the problem. You see, when one feels the need to make others feel inferior to him or her, it signals to me that there is a deficit or an inferiority in *that* person's own life that he or she is attempting to address. By regarding a stranger—a Black stranger—as being "less than," it is because the offender has been made to feel "less than" in some aspect of his or her own life, or maybe there is a feeling of resentment or envy of that Black woman who has the versatile hair or the darker skin and the fuller lips that were not achieved by tanning beds or injections. Perhaps the sight of a Black person is a subconscious reminder of what that person is not. Or is it that my Black life and my presence are simply repulsing? Or is it because you believe you are above me and acknowledging my presence is beneath you. NEWS FLASH!: If you really are "all that," then you know that to acknowledge others demonstrates to the world that you do indeed have it "goin' on."

When one attempts to ignore my existence, I feel sorrow for that person. How that must hurt to will oneself to shift into such a negative mindset. I truly wish for those people a means for filling up themselves so as to eradicate that inner-demand and the fruitless attempts at reducing in the worth and existence of others. I truly wish for them the ability to look and smile at everyone they encounter because when you smile, it automatically demonstrates to the world your strength, your magic, and your power. It automatically demonstrates to the world that you are loved. When you cannot (or refuse to) smile or when you insist on refusing to acknowledge others, it demonstrates _____.

(Un)intentional, (In)direct, and Subtle/Not So Subtle Discrimination
Bridgett recalls questioning if a comment is a compliment or a microaggression.

After making a presentation, I have had White people ask me, "Who does your PowerPoint slides?" My immediate response is a cheerful "Oh! Do you like them?!" I ask this to get a sense of the spirit in which the question is coming, and the answer I receive is always one that's in the affirmative, which prompts me to think Why can it not be assumed that since I am the one who delivered the presentation that I am the one who made the slide deck?

Is the assumption that a Black person cannot have the ability to design a good-looking slide deck? If the message is meant to convey that you like the slides, then why can you not simply say "I like your slides" or "Those are some great-looking slides you made!"? Then the latter statement puts me in a position to confirm or deny whether I created the deck.

Or is the assumption that perhaps I am too busy to design my decks; therefore, a member of my team must design them? That could be. Or is the person wanting to enlist whoever is the designer of my decks to perform work for him/her? Possibly.

But … the conversations have never gone in any of those directions, so I am back to square one—that it is a microaggression, (un)intentional, (in)direct, and subtle or not so subtle discrimination against me, a Black person—that it is not possible for a Black person to be able to design, on her own, such good-looking slide decks.

"You Sure Are Articulate"

Bridgett describes an encounter all too familiar to the countless Blacks who choose to use proper enunciation, intonations, and pacing, while simultaneously speaking grammatically correct English.

As I was on my way to exit a local restaurant after facilitating a meeting, I recognized a retired NBA player sitting at the bar in his usual spot, but this time instead of sitting alone or with his daughter, a White man accompanied him. As I usually do, I stopped to chat before making my way to the parking lot, and the White man was introduced to me as a friend of the retiree's. The conversation wound its way around to the White man telling me, in a complimentary tone, that I was articulate.

At this point, I'd been a business owner for just over three years. I am led to think my age and being my own boss positioned me to have more confidence in speaking my mind. So when he said, "Well, you sure are articulate," I felt a little catch in my throat, knowing four little words had been omitted—"for a Black woman." I paused for a beat, silently composed myself, then calmly responded with "If I was White, would you have said that?"

He, too, had to pause for a moment before responding "No," and it was clear this was a surprise for him. It was clear that he would not have recognized what he just did had I not brought it to his attention.

And I give him credit for taking a contemplative pause. He did not appear taken aback, nor did he appear offended. In that moment, I'd like to think he recalled conversations he had had with Whites and realized he had never openly recognized them for their articulateness, so why, then, was he recognizing me for mine? In that moment, I'd like to think he realized how his comment, albeit complimentary in his mind, made me feel. I'd like to think that in that moment, he made a vow to himself that he would never utter those words to another Black person.

Driving Too Slowly While Black

Bridgett recounts one of her encounters with police in Arizona.

In December 2010, I was stopped by the police for driving too slowly in the vicinity of my and my husband's neighborhood. I did not initially know that was the reason for the stop—the officer did not tell me that was the reason for the stop—but in retrospect, that was the absurd conclusion I drew for why I had been stopped. Nonetheless, I had a feeling I knew why I was being pulled over, but speed had nothing to do with it.

With silent agitation, I let down my window, then retrieve my license from my wallet and dig around in my console for my registration. Once the officer arrives at the side of my car and makes the request for the documents, with visible annoyance but without a word, I flippantly hand them out the window. Neither of us greets each other, and I refuse to make eye contact because I am thoroughly perturbed.

(As I write this and reflect on the stop, I think of how my response is totally different now. The last time I recall getting stopped by police was in 2018, and there is a marked difference in my attitude and behavior from 2010, prior to seeing so many Blacks getting killed by police, to 2018. At that 2018 stop, I promptly and carefully let down my window with minimal movement, put both my hands on the steering wheel so they are visible to the officer, and wait for the officer to appear at the side of my car. At this point, I request permission to reach into my purse and the console to retrieve my license and registration. To the non-Black reader, this may sound ridiculous and hyperbolic. Do know it feels and sounds absolutely ridiculous to *me* to be an adult in America in my own vehicle, asking someone else if it's okay to make a move. However, given the police shooting data and given I am a Black person in this country, in the year 2020, this is what I believe I must do to improve the likelihood I am able to leave the traffic stop alive.)

Again, I *think* have an idea of why my morning agenda has been interrupted by the police but am still surprised there is no explanation for why I have been pulled over in the plaza just around the corner from our home.

The officer returns to my car and starts questioning from whence I was coming and where I was going. (Really?!) "I just left the gym and am on my way home." (In retrospect, this question deeply bothers me because the real question is, "What are you doing here?" or "Why are you, a Black person, in this area?")

He goes on with, "I pulled you over because your driving was suspicious. Even when I would slow down, you would also slow down and wouldn't pass me."

My silent response was "You're absolutely correct. I did not want to be bothered by police today, so I did not want to pass you, possibly inadvertently exceed the speed limit, and find myself where I am now—sitting, pulled over in a parking lot, and starting my day with a citation."

Instead, I offered a response that was something to the effect of, "I was distracted, thinking about my husband who was at home sick with a cold." Weak—I know.

He returns to his cruiser and is in it for some time—an *extremely* long time. I decide he will run my license and registration with the hopes of finding something—*ANYthing*—to make this stop worth his while since speaking with me yields nothing.

17

I do not recall how much time lapses, but he finally returns to the car with my documents and hands them over to me through my open window. Before he walks off, he observes a smidgen of my front left tire protruding over onto a line demarcating a parking space reserved for handicap drivers and abruptly tells me "And don't park in handicap parking spaces."

Really?!

That's all you've got?

Are you feeling defeated?

Is that your one-uppance?

Is that the best you can do?

I roll my eyes and go on about my way.

The sad part is he was so consumed with the hopes of nailing me with a citation, thinking I was concealing an egregious illegality, that he missed the obvious.

My driver's license clearly notates the date of issuance is November 2009; here it is December 2010, thirteen months later, and I still have a Texas license plate on my car. If a citation had been issued for my failure to transfer car registration, which is what I thought was going to happen, then I could not have been mad. He would have been doing his job.

My issue is why choose *my* car—why choose me with whom to play a game of cat and mouse? Out of all the other cars on the road that weekday morning during the 8 a.m. hour when plenty of others are out and on their way to work and school, why choose a BMW 750Li with a Black woman behind the steering wheel to engage in a game of "let me accelerate for the purpose of seeing if the motorist will pass me"? We live in a state where Blacks are currently 4.1% of the population, so I am likely the minority on the road. (And granted, my 750 was not on the level of a Rolls-Royce or a Maserati, but it wasn't your average everyday sedan either.)

Why my car, and why me, a Black woman, in the vicinity of my own neighborhood where my husband and I are homeowners?

Of course, he has no idea if I live in the area or not. And one might ask "What does that matter anyway?" My response is you would think you can easily and comfortably exist in your own neighborhood without being stopped for what ostensibly amounts to nonsense. You would think. (As a matter of fact, when we first moved from Texas to Arizona, Aaron was also stopped for driving too slowly in our neighborhood. The officer indicated he looked suspicious when all he was doing was driving and taking in the area that we had, just days before, decided to call home. Would he have been stopped if he was White?)

Could my December 2010 stop have been random selection? Yes. Do I question it several years later? Obviously. Or…was he simply doing his job?

She Needed Help, Not Handcuffs
Bridgett recalls a neighbor's call to police.

In the summer of 2018, just feet from our front door, I was proud to see a police officer arrive on the scene, assess the situation, avoid any influence from the "excited" neighbor who had put in the call, and set about to do his job.

As I turn on to our street, I see two neighbors, who are university professors, standing in their driveway and a third neighbor, who is a retiree, on his phone, appearing to have an exercised conversation while standing behind a car that's come to a stop in the middle of the street. This is very very very strange. I slowly roll up to the professors and ask "What's going on here?"

They tell me the retiree was on the phone with the police, then give me the backstory: The lady in the car, a Black senior citizen had shown up at the professors' home, asking if they were "the ones with a room for rent." Confused because they were not renting out any part of their home, they told her she was mistaken; however, she allegedly would not leave their front porch. Unsure of what to do, they contacted the retiree, who lives two doors down, and his solution was to call the police. And they seem as perplexed as me regarding his energy on the phone.

I slowly pass the car and the retiree, park my car in our driveway two houses down, and walk back to the scene. I ask the retiree, whom I consider a friend, the exact same question—"What's going on?" He tells me he's on with the police because she won't leave, not that he's on the phone with police "because she needs help." His attitude is clearly one of "she does not belong here." Oookaaay. It's obvious he's not about to hear a thing I might have to say.

My attention then turns to the lady sitting in the car. After introducing myself and asking her name and how I can help her, it is instantly obvious she is disoriented and needs help. The street for which she was looking is not in our neighborhood, written in a little tablet is an incomplete phone number that supposedly belongs to the person she was trying to meet to further inquire about renting a room, and the name of the person for whom she was looking is not the name of anyone I know on our street. From this brief conversation and simply seeing the out-of-state plates on the car she was driving, the walker in her back seat, and her advanced age, she undoubtedly is not a threat that needs removing, and she certainly needs help, not handcuffs. Thank goodness an incredibly kind and professional officer arrived, instantly realized that, and commenced offering assistance. (Drawing conclusions about the neighbor—fairly or unfairly—the officer went so far as to ask about my well-being as a resident in the neighborhood.) However, my mind cannot help but to go to the land of "What if?" There is no question of the possibility that this scenario could have ended totally differently.

My disappointment with the neighbor was not because he called the police. It was because his call appeared to come not from a place of human kindness or compassion but from a place of entitlement or even anger. "How dare this woman come into our neighborhood and refuse to leave! She must go, and she must go now!" is the energy I was getting from the retiree. I have been wanting to talk to him so he can tell me my assessment was wrong, that he was indeed trying to get help for the lady and that I misinterpreted his mannerisms, but I have never found the time nor the energy.

I recall a failed conversation over Thanksgiving dinner circa 2015 when the conversation worked its way around to my insistence that if a situation in the neighborhood ever arose with my and my husband's Black son, then I would want a neighbor to call me, not the police. That conversation, his inability (or lack of a desire) to hear or see my point of view, and his decision to call the police on someone who clearly needed help left me with little hope that speaking with him again about my perspectives regarding the intersection of Blacks and police would yield a different result.

My hope is if the neighbor ever finds himself in a predicament, that he is so fortunate as to have someone show him a little understanding.

Missing Sidewalks, Melted Ice Cream, and Weapons Drawn

Aaron recalls his first encounter with police in Houston and a second encounter that forever changed how he views members of law enforcement.

When I was fourteen is the first time I can remember having my first interaction with the police. It was 1993. We didn't have sidewalks leading to our house, and a group of us—black and brown teenagers—were walking, got pulled over by a Black police officer, and were given citations for walking in the street.

I thought that was the most ridiculous thing in the world.
The judge was of the same mind.

She was incredulous and responded with, "You all missed school for this?!"

And in the same breath, without a moment's hesitation, she issued her ruling.

"Dismissed."

She then turned her attention to the officer. "You are here to protect and serve, not to give citations to teenagers for not walking on sidewalks when there *are* no sidewalks on which to walk. What are they supposed to do? There are no sidewalks. Were they impeding traffic?"

I don't recall the officer's response; he likely had no words. That was just the start of ridiculous encounters I would have with police.

The next one I can recall was about six years later, in July of 1999. I had just turned twenty the month before and was driving to work in my dad's 1974 Chevy pickup truck, which I also shared with my older brother, when I noticed a police car pulling out of the parking lot of a gas station behind me where I'd just fueled up and where

I had also purchased some ice cream. He likely just was going in the same direction I was going, but it was when I dropped some of that ice cream on my pants that everything changed.

When I got to Grant Road, I made a left, then I made a right on Lockwood. The police cruiser is still behind me. I continue on to the Beltway 8 to make a left turn, and that's when I see his lights are on. Quite frankly, I really didn't think the lights were for me, and I pulled over to let him go on his way.

Was I ever so wrong because, at this point, there was a police car coming from the east, another one from the west, and then there was the one behind me. I had been driving for five or six miles at that point, but less than a mile after leaving the store, I swerved because I had spilled ice cream on my khaki pants. And come to find out, therein was the problem—a swerve I made as a result of the spilled ice cream.

He asked me to stick my hands out the window, but there was another problem. I couldn't let down the window: the window crank was broken off. We're talking about a twenty-five-year-old truck here.

At this point, all of the police are out of their cars with guns drawn trained on me.

At this point, I am scared.

I am really scared.

Twice, he told me to put my hands out the window.

Twice, I yelled that I couldn't.

Thanks to the design of this older truck, I was able to open the little triangle window that you don't see on today's models and stick my hands out of it.

Seeing my hands and hopefully getting a sense that I was trying to comply, he approached my door and tried to open it but couldn't. I had to open it from the inside. Again, it's a 1974 truck.

Now, there is a total of five officers on the scene. I have one behind me with a gun, one in front, one to right, and the first officer, all with guns drawn. The fifth one did not have a gun drawn.

"Why did you pull me over?" I ask.
At this point, he puts down his weapon, as do the other officers, and says, "License and registration."

Not until he returns with my license and registration does he tell me that he pulled me over for the swerve, suspecting me of driving while under the influence.

I had my ice cream on the side and a big mess in my lap, which he finally noticed. You could see the embarrassment in his face. He went and gave the other officers the lay of the land, and they left the scene.

However, he went back to his cruiser and stayed for forty minutes or so. I think he just went back and turned on his AC, which was further infuriating, given that my AC didn't work.

Then, all of a sudden, he appeared and said "You're free to go. Just make sure you don't swerve."

Are you kidding me?!

I ended up getting pulled over, having MULTIPLE guns drawn on me, getting scared out of my mind, and being forty minutes late for work, and that's what you tell me?!

24

When I arrived to work my shift at the department store and explained my delay, my supervisor asked in astonishment, "*You* got pulled over? That's not like you. You're a clean-cut guy who gets from point A to point B without bothering anyone. Did you get a ticket?"

"No."

"Hmm…the cop must have been having a bad day."

The Black coworkers instantly saw it differently.

And even getting a newer truck didn't help. I remember when I first purchased my 2007 pickup truck, which I still own (and will likely keep for twenty-five years!), that I was pulled over and asked for my license and registration. The officer asked me from where I had gotten the truck. I showed him my bill of sale bearing my name, at which point he said a truck similar to mine had been reported stolen. Really? There are tons of white trucks on the road.

That experience from 1999 causes me to have anxiety whenever I see police, especially if I know I haven't done anything. That shouldn't be. Sadly, my father once told me that when I'm approached by the police to just comply. "Son, just go along with whatever they say, even if you know they are wrong." Again, that should not be.

The police officer who pulled me over in 1999 patrolled that neighborhood on the regular. He saw (or should have noticed) that truck I was driving at least twice a week. The one thing you knew about that truck was it was never driven over the speed limit and it was driven by two young men: my older brother and me.

I don't think he understood the community he patrolled, which is a working-class community.

He overused his power by calling all his comrades, and he held me on the side of the road in a way that felt like a punishment, given it was July in Houston and I had no working A/C.
If his true intent was to serve and protect, then the first thing he could have said was, "Hey. I saw you swerved. I just wanted to perform a safety check on you and ensure you're okay."

I still cannot get over that. It was over twenty years ago, and I still can't get over that.

This was a time before cell phones were popular, so there was no calling anyone or commencing a Facebook Live stream.

I was scared. I did not know what had happened that made them pull me over. The only thing I knew to do was to do what they asked me to do or to at least try my best to be compliant so they would not hurt me.

Both the Police AND YOU Are Responsible for How It Goes Down
Bridgett asserts that everyone plays a role in how encounters with police can play out.

It does not matter whether you *think* you are not doing anything wrong or not. It does not matter if you feel inconvenienced or that your day has been interrupted. It does not matter if you have a dislike for law enforcement; are in a rush; are tired, frustrated, annoyed, or are minding your own business. It does not matter. If someone in authority—specifically, the police—issues a command, comply. Period. Do not provoke; do not give any reason for the situation to escalate.

Simply comply.

This is not about acquiescing. This is not about becoming subservient. This is not about relinquishing your power. This is about respecting someone in authority—a concept we were taught (or should have been taught) early on in our homes. If your parent told you to do something, you did it with no questions asked. Your parent was the governing body of that home and was the one who laid down the law. It was a matter of respect. You did as you were told. End of story. Apply a similar attitude here.

Police are present to make sense of a situation that, upon first glance, can appear senseless. They arrive on a scene with limited intel and must make life-or-death decisions with expediency and with the intent of serving and protecting. We, as citizens, make it easier on everyone if we simply do what we are asked or told to do.

One cannot expect a smooth, uneventful outcome if asked by police to stop, drop, sit down, turn around, discontinue talking, stop moving, etc. if one fails to act as directed. Can it feel infuriating for someone to bark orders at you? Yes. Might one feel disrespected if yelled at? Sure. Are you concerned about being in the wrong place at the wrong time with a criminal record that may not bode well for you? Prepare to face the music. An active scene with police on the job, working to ascertain who is the aggressor and who is the victim is not the place for pleasantries and a chat over a spot o' tea and crumpets. This is but one moment in time. Listen, check the attitude, respond appropriately, and recognize it is more about resolving a matter than it is about you feeling disrespected; embracing these fundamental points can make the difference between increasing the chances of you getting on your way or increasing the chances of the encounter evolving into a less than desirable one. Moreover, if you have an officer who is equally overly concerned with receiving respect, then you are faced with a "¿Quién es más macho?" ("Who is more macho?") scenario. Then, who wins?

Are there intervening circumstances that may impede one's ability to comply, e.g., mental illness, physical limitations, or medical conditions? Absolutely. And in those instances, police need to be equipped with the training and/or the resources to recognize when that may be the case so they can respond in a way that brings to the setting assistance as opposed to aggression.

We all own a role in what happens during a police stop. All of the duty to act civilly and responsibly does not solely lie with the police. It is a joint effort.

What Needs to Change
Aaron explains the differences that need to come about for police and communities.

Police need improved training that includes comprehensive diversity components, and police departments need to hire people who know and live in the neighborhoods they patrol. And if they do not live in the neighborhood, then they need to attend events in that neighborhood. Get to know who lives there, and learn how the people act.

Understand you can have two Black men who are talking loudly to each other, and that's just the way they interact with each other. They are not angry. They are not about to go to blows. And you know that because you know your community.

If it's a blue-collar neighborhood, then people might cuss and fuss. That's just what they do!

And if you know the community, then you will know if there are sidewalks or not.

If you see a man in the same car every day at 4 p.m. going to work with a uniform on, then he is not a threat, especially if he's pulling away from a gas station with a pint of ice cream, not a pint of liquor.

If you have to pull over somebody, then refrain from being so aggressive, thinking you need to dominate the person in the car. You are already in a dominant position in that you are wearing a badge. You can say a greeting, state what you observed, and ask for the driver's license and registration.

Get educated about the neighborhood. Spend time in the neighborhoods you police and actually get to know the residents. In the neighborhood where I grew up, there were about a hundred homes, and at least 70% of them had school-age children. Get to know those children! The only time I remember seeing police at our school was on career day. That's insufficient. Let us see you and get to know you before you harass us about walking in the street because we are not walking on sidewalks that do not exist.

Put in place a system where police are not instantly called for every instance of a nonviolent incident, such as a person asleep in his car in a fast food drive-through, as was the case with the killing of Rayshard Brook by police in Georgia, or a patron allegedly passing or attempting to pass a counterfeit bill at a point of sale in a store, as has been reported in the killing of George Floyd by police in Minnesota.

Now, what is life like to leave home not knowing what you will face at the "office," an office that is the streets of a city where you are tasked with keeping law and order and upholding a promise to serve and protect? Your goal is to do your job to the best of your ability and return home safe and sound at the end of your shift.

Unless you are a police officer, you cannot fully appreciate or understand the weight of that reality. We cannot begin to pretend to know what that life is like.

Because of the work the police do, the rest of us are free to enjoy our liberties and walk the streets feeling we are safe. When they approach any situation, they have to assume the worst. It is the premise under which they must operate by virtue of wearing the badge and the uniform. They have to know and believe they are in place to keep or restore peace. They have to be on guard and ready for anything. They know nothing about the person in the car, on the sidewalk, on the street. Nothing. Can you imagine working a job where terror could be around any corner?! They have to put so much into motion when they are faced with a situation: judgment, sensibility, heightened awareness of how their actions will impact everyone…. It's complex, and we can only imagine. The choice is either "I go home alive, or I don't."

At the same time, there are those instances where it seems judgment, sensibility, and a heightened awareness for how their actions will impact everyone get lost, and we all suffer.

For those members of law enforcement who truly do honor the badge, who show each day to serve and protect, and who do so no matter the color of a person's skin, the socioeconomic conditions of the neighborhood, or the character of its citizens, we thank you. We thank you for being strong, brave pillars of your communities. We thank you for putting us in a position to be able to live freely. We thank you for risking your own safety for the safety of our families and friends. And we ask that if you *see* something that you also *say* something. Speak up and act when you know a colleague's actions are questionable and may put a life in danger.

We Are Not Angry…We Are Tired: A Journey of 400+ Years

Aaron and Bridgett provide a history of Blacks in America based on hours and hours of research, and they include sparing personal commentary to offer evidence for not only the exhaustion of Blacks but also the need to keep moving forward.

In early June of 2020, we received phone calls, text messages, and email messages from seven friends and associates who were concerned about us—seven: a techie in

California; a naturopathic doctor, a financial advisor, and a sales and marketing professional in Arizona; an expat and podcaster in Michigan; an educator in Texas; and a sales expert in Colorado. They were great conversations. And we are so appreciative to them for picking up the phone or logging on to see if we were okay and to ask us thoughtful questions in the midst of the news, protests, and demonstrations taking place around the world in the wake of George Floyd's murder at the hands of police. We were grateful for the seven calls we received but were disappointed that there were not more calls or messages. We were further disappointed that when the protests, demonstrations, and news coverage ceased, so did the conversations. We quietly transitioned into a business-as-usual state of mind.

Oftentimes, because there is already so much frustration and fatigue from living the life of a Black person day in and day out, some Blacks are numb and just don't say anything. Some are upset. Others are offended. Others are annoyed.

We live that life every single day and may or may not speak up if there is a slight, a microaggression, an instance of racism. But we hear you. We hear you and we see you. We may not say anything, but we hear you and we see you.

And for those who want to learn more, who ask us questions for the sake of better understanding who we are, we see you, too. And we thank you. If our responses to your queries and curiosity seem a little abrasive or abrupt at times, do not take it personally, and please do not call us angry.

We are not angry.

You do not want to see us angry. Trust and believe. You do not want to see us angry.

Simply put, we are tired. What you see is exhaustion. Over 400 years of exhaustion.

To understand the fear, frustration, and exhaustion, we must review and understand Blacks' history in this nation.

In **August of 1619,** *The White Lion* ship lands at the port in Jamestown, Virginia, loaded with more than twenty of our ancestors from Africa, who were exchanged for food and money. This was the start of the American slave trade.

By **June of 1640,** Virginia's General Court creates what many call the colonies' first law establishing slavery. John Punch, one of the Africans who arrived aboard *The White Lion*, ran away from his master along with an indentured Dutch servant and an indentured English servant. When they were found and returned to their master, a judge ordered the whipping of each one. But the equal treatment stopped there. The Dutchman and the Englishmen each received a one-year extension on their indentured servitude contracts; however, John Punch was sentenced to a life of servitude.

In **1669,** Virginia's legislature passes a law wherein masters can kill their slaves as a means of punishing them and not face any legal repercussions. The point was clear: they could subjectively murder another human being—a Black human being—with no fear of consequences.

In **1704**, South Carolina creates "slave patrols" whose responsibilities include chasing down, capturing, and returning runaway slaves to their owners and providing organized terror as a means of deterring slaves from revolting. In short, the message to enslaved Blacks was stay in your place. Don't even think of leaving. It doesn't matter how hard life is, how unfair life is, how degrading life is—if you try to leave, then you will get hunted down and returned to that life. No questions asked.

In **1712,** the New York Slave Revolt is an uprising where twenty enslaved Africans kill nine Whites and injure another six before they are stopped. Of the total seventy Black people who were arrested and jailed, twenty-seven were put on trial and twenty-one were convicted and executed. (This was not the first slave rebellion in the United States, nor would it be the last. And how can anyone blame them for rejecting their enslavement? San Miguel de Gualdape, a colony founded in **1526** on the coast of Georgia, was the first European settlement in what became the continental United States but lasted less than four months from being overwhelmed by disease, hunger, and a Native American population who responded hostilely toward the colonizers. The enslaved Africans brought by the settlers became the first documented instance of Black slavery in North America and led to the first slave rebellion.)

In **April 1740,** South Carolina passes The Negro Law of 1740, which makes it illegal for enslaved Africans to leave the colonies, assemble in groups, grow food, earn money, or learn to write. It was this law that gave slave owners, for the next 125 years, the right to kill rebellious slaves. So, let us be very clear about what has happened here: Blacks have no power and no rights whatsoever in this land, can be killed for reacting with insolence as any human would, but they are not allowed to leave this land without facing consequences.

On **March 5, 1770,** Crispus Attucks, a stevedore of African and Native American descent, is the first American killed in the Boston Massacre and thus the first American killed in the American Revolution. This happened when America's first police brutality protest turned into a riot as British troops, responsible for policing colonists, opened fire on Boston residents..

In **1777,** Vermont, which was not a state at the time, becomes the first territory to abolish slavery, and in **1780,** while still a territory, Pennsylvania follows suit. Then in **1781**, New York voted to free slaves who fought with the rebels during the Revolutionary War. It's feeling like there's progress in the right direction until six years later, when Blacks were hit with the Constitution's ratification, with its Three-Fifths Compromise.

In **1787,** enslaved Blacks count as three-fifths of a person for the purpose of determining a state's total population for legislative representation and taxing purposes. This relegation is meant to address the apportionment in the US House of Representatives and the number of electoral votes each state would have in presidential elections based on a state's population.

Article I, Section 2 of the US Constitution states "Representatives and direct Taxes shall be apportioned among the several States which may be included within this Union, according to their respective Numbers, which shall be determined by adding to the whole Number of free Persons, including those bound to Service for a Term of Years, and excluding Indians not taxed, three fifths of all other Persons."

The "other Persons" were slaves.

Some will argue that counting the whole number of slaves would have given the Southern states an unfair advantage, that it would have allowed for further and continued perpetuation of the institution of slavery, and that minimizing the percentage of the slave population counted for apportionment reduced slaveholding states' political power. However, others will argue that the act of changing the status of a human being so that he or she is counted as three-fifths of a person—no matter the reason, and even it helps lead to that person's freedom—is degrading and signals a regard for the life of those persons as having less significance in comparison to other humans. Given all that had happened to enslaved Blacks in this country up to that point, they had been made to feel and had been treated as being less than human; now it was documented on paper that, for whatever reason, they would be counted as less than a full human.

With the intent of allaying fears of any armed Black uprisings, in **December of 1791,** Congress ratifies the Second Amendment to the Constitution so Americans can have the right to bear arms.

Then, on **February 12, 1793**, President George Washington signs into law the Fugitive Slave Clause of the US Constitution, which requires officials from free states to assist slave holders or their agents in recapturing runaway, or fugitive, slaves. The clause was later superseded by the Thirteenth Amendment, but that wouldn't happen until more than seventy years later. If a law is required to insist that a people remain in your country, then that is extremely problematic.

Decades before, Vermont and Pennsylvania were on the right track with abolishing slavery, and President George Washington signed into law on **March 22, 1794,** the Slave Trade Act of 1794, which made it illegal for Americans to outfit ships for purpose of importing slaves. During the eighteenth century alone, it is estimated that Africa was deprived of six to seven million of its healthiest and ablest men and women, who were imported to and enslaved in the New World.

In yet another step in the right direction, The Act Prohibiting the Importation of Slaves of 1807 takes effect on **January 1, 1808,** after which no new slaves could be imported to the United States.

But this is not enough. On **August 21, 1831,** Nat Turner leads the only effective slave rebellion in United States history. On that night, he and a small band of followers killed his owners, the Travis family, and set off toward the town of Jerusalem, Virginia. Over the course of two days, before being suppressed, the group of around seventy-five Blacks killed approximately sixty White people. Turner escaped but was captured six weeks later and was tried and hanged.

Starting in **1810,** decades before Nat Turner's Revolt, and lasting until **1850,** the Underground Railroad is in operation. It consisted of abolitionists, freed Blacks, Whites, and enslaved workers who operated a network of secret routes and safe houses that were used by enslaved Blacks to escape into free states, Canada, and Mexico. Born Araminta Ross, Harriet Tubman was the Underground Railroad's most famous conductor and is credited with making some thirteen missions to rescue approximately seventy enslaved people.

And while there is freedom for some Blacks, it is not 100% freedom. This is evidenced when on **March 6, 1857,** after suing for his freedom on the grounds that he and his wife had for years lived in a free state, Dred Scott receives a ruling from Chief Justice Roger Taney in *Dred Scott v. Sanford* that declares Scott had no grounds on which to sue because he was a Black man, and as a Black person, he was not an American. The court held that no persons of African descent, including slaves and free persons, could ever become citizens of the United States. Referencing the clause in the Declaration of Independence that "all men are created equal," Taney wrote "It is too clear for dispute, that the enslaved African race were not intended to be included, and formed no part of the people who framed and adopted this declaration." He went on to add that "Black Americans…had no rights which the White man was bound to respect."

While the Slave Trade Act of 1794 and The Act Prohibiting the Importation of Slaves of 1807 are in full effect, on **April 12, 1861,** eleven slave-holding states that are not fine with eliminating enslavement of humans secede from the country to form their own confederacy. The Confederate States of America was organized in rebellion against the US Constitution. The remaining twenty-three states remained loyal to the United States and were known as the Union. What followed was the

Civil War, in which 620,000 to 750,000 people were killed, making it the bloodiest war in American history.

On **September 22, 1862**, President Abraham Lincoln issues the preliminary Emancipation Proclamation, which declares that as of **January 1, 1863,** all enslaved people in the states currently engaged in rebellion against the Union "shall be then, thenceforward, and forever free." So while the argument is quite accurate that the Civil War was about more than slavery, the Emancipation Proclamation legally recognized that the Civil War was indeed fought for slavery and not just to preserve the Union. (On the night of **December 31, 1862,** the tradition of Watch Night Service, which is still observed and practiced in Black churches on New Year's Eve, began when free Blacks living in the Union States gathered at churches and/or other safe spaces, and thousands of enslaved Blacks knelt and prayed on plantations, awaiting word via telegraph, newspaper, or word of mouth that President Lincoln had signed the Emancipation Proclamation into law.)

On **January 1, 1863,** Lincoln does indeed sign the Emancipation Proclamation, but it does not free all of the approximately four million enslaved men, women, and children and applied only to the Confederate states that were in rebellion at the time. Exempt from proclamation were the four border slave states (Delaware, Maryland, Kentucky, and Missouri) and all or parts of three Confederate states controlled by the Union Army.

Not surprisingly, some slave owners kept this from their slaves. To ensure slaves had been freed, government agents traveled the country, asking Blacks questions such as "How are you working?" and "What are you getting?" When any slaves responded that they were not receiving compensation for their work, the agent had the slave owner go before the government.

Southern planters had little to no money and had no slaves, but they needed labor for their plantations. At the same time, most freedmen had no money, food, or clothing and needed all three plus housing.

Former slave owners and plantation owners took advantage of the situation. Many workers received housing, seeds, and credit at a commissary store. The original intent was when the crop was sold, Black workers would share in the crop, but many people engaged in dishonest bookkeeping, thereby causing the former slaves to remain in debt to the plantation owner for years.

On **April 9, 1865,** The American Civil War official ends when General Robert E. Lee surrenders to the Union General Ulysses S. Grant at the Appomattox Court House in Virginia, and slavery is subsequently abolished. The Reconstruction Amendments to the US Constitution (the Thirteenth, Fourteenth, and Fifteenth Amendments) followed and granted emancipation and constitutional rights of citizenship to all Blacks. Blacks were able to vote and hold political office but were increasingly deprived of civil rights, often under Jim Crow laws, and were discriminated against and sustained violence at the hands of White supremacists in the South. Jim Crow laws governed life in the South, requiring the separation of Whites from "persons of color" on public transportation and in schools, parks, restaurants, theaters, and other locations.

On **June 19, 1865,** more than two and a half years after the enactment of President Lincoln's Emancipation that had already freed the slaves, Union soldiers, led by Major General Gordon Granger, land at Galveston, Texas, with news that the Civil War had ended and that the slaves were free. Until then, the Emancipation Proclamation had little impact on Texans because there were not enough Union troops in the area to enforce the law. The holiday, known as Juneteenth, is the oldest nationally celebrated commemoration of the ending of slavery in the United States. (On **July 22, 2020**, a bipartisan attempt to make Juneteenth a federal holiday fails in the US Senate. Rationale for not making June 19 a federal holiday involved money—that it would cost private-sector taxpayers about $600 million on an annual basis to give federal workers this paid day off. [And how much money did America make on the backs of free labor from slaves?!])

The period from **1863** until **1877** is known as the Reconstruction Era, which ended the remnants of Confederate secession and abolished slavery, making the newly freed slaves citizens of the United States with civil rights ostensibly guaranteed by the Thirteenth, Fourteenth, and Fifteenth Amendments to the US Constitution.

On **December 18, 1865**, the Thirteenth Amendment to the US Constitution is adopted and abolishes slavery and involuntary servitude except as a means for punishment for those convicted of crimes. To ensure Blacks did not get too comfortable with this notion of freedom, days later, on **December 24, 1865,** the Ku Klux Klan (KKK) is formed in Pulaski, Tennessee, by six former Confederate soldiers, becoming a vehicle for Southern White underground resistance to Reconstruction with the goal of restoring White supremacy. What was really happening with this assertion of White dominance is that some Whites needed a means for suppressing Blacks out of a fear that Black people would turn on Whites in retaliation for hundreds of years of inhumane, unfair, murderous treatment endured by Blacks. Hundreds of years. White supremacy = fear. Not only do hurt people hurt other people, but those who are scared attempt to scare others.

The country starts to see a proliferation of the establishment of historically Black colleges and universities (HBCUs) to provide Blacks, who up to this point had not been allowed to attend colleges and universities, with a basic education and training to become teachers and tradesmen. Cheyney University, the first historically Black university, is established in Pennsylvania prior to the Civil War in **1837.** The number of HBCUs grew to its highest, at 121, in the 1930s. As of August 2020, there are 101 HBCUs in the country. (Quick note: Given how long HBCUs have been in existence, it is a pity and a shame the number of times we have had to explain to non-Black Americans what "HBCU" stands for.)

With the purpose of enforcing the Thirteenth Amendment and protecting the rights of Black Americans, Congress creates and enacts the Civil Rights Act of 1866 on **April 9, 1866,** but it is not ratified until 1870. It was the first federal law that defined citizenship and affirmed that all citizens are equally protected by the law. President Andrew Johnson vetoed the bill, and although Congress successfully overrode Johnson's veto and made it into law in April 1866 some Republicans thought another amendment was necessary; therefore, on **July 9, 1868,** the Fourteenth Amendment is ratified, making former enslaved Africans citizens of the United States and voiding the 1857 Dred Scott ruling. Once again, the KKK was not having this—this notion of Blacks getting closer and closer to truly being recognized for the humans that they are and regarded as equal citizens in this country—so from that date until 1877, the KKK and other Whites organized and put into effect a national terror campaign that results in the killings of tens of thousands of Blacks in the United States.

Between **1868** and **1870**, the KKK reaches its peak. Klan members dressed in robes and sheets designed to scare Blacks and to prevent federal troops from identifying them whipped and brutally killed freed Blacks and their White supporters during nighttime raids. Believed to have been the KKK's first grand wizard, General Nathan Bedford Forrest ordered the KKK's disbandment in **1869**, citing the group's excessive violence as the primary reason for the order, but local branches continued the terror. Therefore, the Enforcement Act of 1870, also known as the Civil Rights Act of 1870, the First KKK Act, or Force Act, was enacted on **May 31, 1870** and went into effect in 1871; it was a federal law that, in part, authorized the president to suppress disturbances by force and impose heavy penalties upon terrorist organizations.

While the *United States v. Harris* decision declares the Ku Klux Klan Act unconstitutional in a **January 22, 1883,** ruling, the Klan had all but disappeared by then because its ultimate goal of achieving White supremacy throughout the South had been achieved.

On **February 3, 1870,** the third and final Reconstruction Era amendment, the Fifteenth Amendment, becomes law and prohibits the federal government and each state from denying a citizen the right to vote based on "race, color, or previous condition of servitude."

But from **the late 1870s** until the hard-won successes of the civil rights movement of the **1960s,** Jim Crow laws govern Black life in the South, requiring the separation of Whites from "persons of color" in nearly all public locations.

In **January of 1877**, Rutherford B. Hayes loses the popular vote to Democrat Samuel J. Tilden but wins the electoral-college vote after the Congressional commission awards him twenty contested electoral votes. The Republican Party's Hayes, a lawyer and staunch abolitionist, pushed through the Compromise of 1877, which resulted in the South being left to govern itself. More specifically, as the nineteenth President of the United States, Hayes agreed to withdraw troops from the South, thereby ending US Army support for Republican state governments, in turn ending support for freed Blacks to establish their families and live as free citizens and ending the Reconstruction Era.

The end of federal interference in southern affairs led to widespread disenfranchiseement of Black voters.

The Fourteenth Amendment is put to the test on **May 18, 1896,** when the United States Supreme Court, in *Plessy v. Ferguson,* upholds a Louisiana law requiring the segregation of passengers on railroad cars. It found that as long as the railroad cars provided both groups with reasonably equal conditions, then the equal-protection clause was not violated.

While segregation took a forceful hold in the South at the close of the nineteenth century, many Blacks looked to self-improvement through education as a means for escaping indignities they endured. Booker T. Washington, the author of *Up From Slavery* and the president of Alabama's Normal and Industrial Institute, was one such source of inspiration. Another was George Washington Carver, a formerly enslaved Black and the head of Tuskegee Institute's agriculture department. And a third was Harvard-educated historian, sociologist, and author of *Souls of Black Folk*, W. E. B. Du Bois, who became a leading voice in the growing Black protest movement during the first half of the twentieth century.

In **June 1905,** Du Bois leads a group that meets at Niagara Falls, Canada, to form the Niagara Movement, a political protest movement to demand civil rights for Blacks in response to the increased violent hostility toward and lynching of Blacks all around the country. In **1909,** the Niagara Movement combines its agenda with the National Association for the Advancement of Colored People (NAACP), America's oldest and eventually largest civil rights organization, whose goals are to the abolish all forced segregation, advocate for the full and consistent enforcement of the Fourteenth and Fifteenth Amendments, attain education for Black students that is indeed equal to that of what White students enjoy, and secure complete enfranchisement of all Black men.

Blacks continue to struggle with finding their way toward fully realizing all the benefits of American citizenship. In the summer of **1919,** veterans return home from World War I, and Red Summer occurs, an event of racial violence that affects at least twenty-six cities across the United States. White servicemen had had their vacated jobs filled by Blacks. Simultaneously, many Whites feared that the return of tens of thousands of Black veterans would not be willing to resubmit to traditional subjugation in the United States. Due to competition for opportunities plus a new social landscape, Blacks and Whites were placed in a new state of conflict.

This conflict erupts on **May 31, 1921,** when thousands of Whites in Tulsa, Oklahoma, descend on the city's predominantly Black Greenwood District to burn down homes and businesses and kill hundreds of people. The Tulsa Race Massacre started on **May 30,** when Dick Rowland, a Black man, stepped into an elevator in a downtown Tulsa building and was alone in the elevator with its operator, a White woman, Sarah Page, who was heard screaming. One account is that Rowland stepped on Page's foot. Nonetheless, Rowland fled the scene, and the next day, he was arrested. A story published in the *Tulsa Tribune* on May 31 claimed that Rowland attempted to rape Page, and over the next twenty-four hours, thousands of White rioters descended on Greenwood District and burned thirty-five city blocks, including more than 1,200 Black-owned houses, numerous businesses, a school, a hospital, and a dozen churches.

Even more conflict between Whites and Blacks is manifested when, on **January 1, 1923,** Fannie Taylor, a White woman, claims a Black man assaulted her in her home, and she sets in motion the Rosewood Massacre, an attack on Rosewood, Florida, a town predominantly comprised of Blacks. White aggressors completely destroyed the town, and by the end of the violence, the residents were driven out permanently.

During World War II, more than three million Blacks register to serve, and of those three million, approximately 500,000 travel overseas for the war, fighting for what President Franklin D. Roosevelt calls the "Four Freedoms"—freedom of speech, freedom of worship, freedom from want, and freedom from fear, although Blacks had yet to obtain those freedoms in America. Enlisted Blacks and Whites were organized into separate units, causing, in part, difficulty with maintaining high morale among Black forces. In **July 1948**, President Harry S Truman used an executive order to integrate the United States Armed Forces, mandating that "there shall be equality of treatment and opportunity for all persons in the armed services without regard to race, color, religion or national origin."

Legislative efforts continue to unfold in an effort to make Blacks truly equal and fully integrated as citizens of this country. Up until **May 17, 1954,** *Plessy v. Ferguson* has been the precedent in civil rights cases, but that is reversed when, in a unanimous decision, the United States Supreme Court rules in *Brown v. Board of Education of Topeka* that U.S. state laws establishing racial segregation in public schools are unconstitutional. Up to that point, the system of racial separation in schools masqueraded as providing separate but equal treatment of both White and Black Americans while Blacks received inferior accommodations, services, and treatment. While the landmark decision was a victory for Blacks, it did not spell out any kind of concrete plan for actually ending racial segregation in schools (or anywhere else for that matter). This is evidenced when, in **September 1957,** Arkansas Governor Orval Faubus called the Arkansas National Guard to prevent nine Black students from entering Central High School in Little Rock. Faubus was forced to call of the guard, and the country watched the standoff play out on television as White mobs converged on the Little Rock Nine. The contrast between the two groups was striking: angry Whites at the attack and peaceful Blacks under attack. For the first time since Reconstruction, federal troops provide Blacks with protection against racial violence, and the Black students finally enter the school surrounded by heavily armed guards.

While racial segregation is, in theory, no more in schools, that is not the case in all places, namely public transportation. In Montgomery, Alabama, on **December**

1, 1955, seamstress Rosa Parks, who is seated in the "colored section," rejects bus driver James F. Blake's order to give her seat to a White passenger after the Whites-only section becomes fully occupied. She certainly was not the first person to refuse to abide by the rules of segregation, but as the secretary of her local NAACP chapter, the organization saw her as the ideal person to be a leader in supporting its continued quest for equality.

Just over four years later, on **February 1, 1960**, four Black students from the Agricultural and Technical College in Greensboro, North Carolina, also refuse to move. They had seated themselves at Woolworth's lunch counter and ordered coffee. Due to the "Whites only" policy, they were refused service, but they stayed in their seats until the store closed, returning the next day and bringing other students with them. The sit-in received extensive news media coverage, sparking a movement that quickly saw young Blacks and Whites engage in various forms of peaceful protests against segregation in libraries, on beaches, in hotels, and at other public establishments with separate policies for Blacks and Whites. Many protesters were arrested for trespassing, disorderly conduct, or disturbing the peace, but Woolworth's as well as other establishments was eventually forced to change their segregationist policies.

By the early part of the twentieth century, the KKK has gained new life and has a resurgence during the **1960s** with bombings, whippings, and shootings in Southern communities. Again, White supremacy equates to fear. On **May 14, 1961**, Birmingham Alabama police commissioner Bull Connor along with KKK co-conspirators coordinate an attack on Freedom Riders, people who challenge racial laws in the South at the time, specifically by refusing to abide by laws that designate bus seating based on race. Klansmen and recruited racists beat, firebomb, and hospitalize peaceful protesters on a bus near Anniston, Alabama.

Attacks on Black lives are such a reality that American civil rights activist Medgar Evers and his wife, Myrlie, train their children what to do in the event of a bombing or shooting. But no amount of training would have stopped the bullet from the rifle wielded by White Citizens' Council member Byron De La Beckwith that killed Medgar Evers in Evers' own Jackson, Mississippi, driveway the morning of **June 12, 1963.**

Before the summer of 1963 ends, Blacks suffer more loss. On **September 15, 1963,** just weeks after Rev. Dr. Martin Luther King, Jr.'s iconic March on Washington with a quarter of a million Blacks and Whites participating and his stirring words delivered at the Lincoln Memorial, White supremacists bomb the 16th Street Baptist Church in Birmingham, Alabama, killing four Black girls— fourteen-year-olds Addie Mae Collins, Cynthia Wesley, and Carole Robertson, and eleven-year-old Denise McNair—as they were putting on their choir robes.

They were children. In a church. CHILDREN! IN. A. CHURCH!

This was a blatant disregard for the sanctity of the building and that for which it stands and an obvious display of no morality or *basic* empathy for innocent children could have been (and who indeed *were*) inside the building.

On **January 23, 1964**, the ratification of the Twenty-Fourth Amendment meant neither Congress nor the states were allowed to enact poll taxes or require any other payment as a pre-condition to voting. The 1937 Supreme Court ruling in *Breedlove v. Suttles* found poll taxes constitutional, and the laws were in effect in several Southern states in an effort to exclude Black voters who were often times economically disadvantaged and in no position to pay a tax. To avoid disenfranchisement of large number of poor whites, such laws typically included a grandfather clause, which exempted from the tax any adult male whose father or grandfather had previously voted but did not exempt any Black males because no Black fathers or Black grandfathers had been able to vote up to that point. The ratified Twenty-Fourth Amendment meant, going forward, there was to be no payment prerequisite to vote.

The summer of 1964 becomes known as "Freedom Summer." It was on **July 2, 1964** when the Civil Rights Act of 1964 is signed into law by President Lyndon B. Johnson, and Jim Crow laws finally become no more. The act outlawed discrimination based on race, color, religion, sex, or national origin. It prohibited unequal application of voter registration requirements and racial segregation in schools, places of employment, and public places, such as restaurants and retail stores.

In short order, "Freedom Summer" is also met by "Mississippi Burning." Just over a month later, three volunteers—two Whites and one Black—disappear after investigating the burning of a Black church by the KKK. A massive FBI investigation, code-named "Mississippi Burning," leads to discovering their buried bodies in Neshoba County, Mississippi, on **August 4, 1964.** The nineteen offenders, White supremacists who included the county's deputy sheriff, were not arrested by the state. However, the Justice Department indicted them—not for murder but for violating the victims' civil rights—and they went on trial in Jackson, Mississippi. In **October 1967**, nine received acquittals, and the remaining seven received guilty verdicts that result in each man serving no more than six years behind bars.

The KKK continues its violence against and hate for Blacks when, on **March 7, 1965,** also known as Bloody Sunday, Alabama State Troopers and the KKK attack 600 nonviolent protesters, led by Rev. Dr. Martin Luther King, Jr., who were marching from Selma to Montgomery in the name of the right to register and vote without being harassed and in response to the **February 18, 1965,** shooting death by Alabama State Troopers in Marion of Jimmie Lee Jackson, a peaceful demonstrator. (Jackson's murder came three days before the **February 21, 1965,** Nation of Islam assassination of Malcolm X, a Black minister and human rights activist, who is best known for being a vocal spokesman for the Nation of Islam and for being a controversial figure accused, during the civil rights movement, of preaching racism and violence in response to the continued unfair treatment of Blacks and is also known for urging his followers to defend themselves "by any means necessary.")

When attempting to vote, election officials often told Blacks that they had gotten the date, time, or polling place wrong; that they did not possess sufficient literacy skills; or that they had not correctly completed an application. In some instances, they were forced to take literacy tests before they were granted the right to cast their votes, which was a challenge at times due to high rates of illiteracy in the Black population as a result of centuries of oppression and poverty. In other instances, voting officials primarily in Southern states, had been known to require Black voters to recite the entire US Constitution before they were allowed to vote. Bloody Sunday took place on the Edmund Pettus Bridge, which is named for a lawyer and decorated Confederate general who became a US senator and leader in the KKK. This was the first of three marches.

The second one takes place on **March, 9, 1965,** when troopers, police, and marchers confront each other at the county end of the bridge, but when the troopers step aside to let them pass, King leads the marchers back to the church to comply with a federal injunction and to seek protection from federal court for the march. That night, a White group beat and murdered civil rights activist James Reeb, a minister from Boston, who arrived in Selma to march.

It is on **March 21, 1965,** the date of the third march and after Alabama Governor George Wallace refuses to protect them, that President Lyndon B. Johnson commits to do so. The marchers are protected by 1,900 members of the Alabama National Guard under federal command as well as FBI agents and federal marshals. The marchers average ten miles a day along US Route 80, arriving in Montgomery on **March 24**. The following year, on **August 6, 1965,** the Voting Rights Act becomes law, prohibiting racial discrimination in voting.

On **April 4, 1968,** in Memphis Tennessee, Rev. Dr. Martin Luther King, Jr. is assassinated, sparking riots in over 100 cities across the nation.

Nearly twenty-five years later, on **January 18, 1993,** for the first time, every state in the United States observes the federal holiday Martin Luther King, Jr. Day, which is observed on the third Monday of January. (On **November 2, 1983,** President Ronald Reagan signed a bill into law, creating the federal holiday to honor King. The final vote in the House of Representatives was on **August 2, 1983;** the final vote in the Senate was on **October 19, 1983;** and the holiday was observed for the first time on **January 20, 1986.**)

On **March 3, 1991**, one of the first viral police brutality videos captures four Los Angeles Police Department officers beating Rodney King, and on **April 21, 1992,** a jury acquits the four officers. Riots ensue.

Then, on **February 4, 1999,** the shooting of Amadou Diallo, a twenty-year-old Guinean immigrant, by four plain-clothes New York City police officers becomes the first in a series of dozens of reports on the deaths of Black men, women, and children who meet their demise far too soon and with far too many questions surrounding whether their race was a factor in their deaths, and we are reminded of the death of these three children who did not have the benefit of police body cameras or bystanders recording cell phone video footage to document the final moments of their lives that were lost at the hands of police:

Randolph Evans, 15, on November 25, 1976
Claude Reese, 14, on September 15, 1974
Clifford Glover, 10, on April 28, 1973

In order for life to get better, for the future for our children to shine as brightly as possible, in order for justice to occur, we must speak up. We must tell anyone who will listen why we are tired.

We are tired and are fearful that we will read or see another news story that is a reminder of the fates met by:

Amadou Diallo, 23, on February 4, 1999
Timothy Stansbury, Jr., 19, on January 24, 2004
Sean Bell, 23, on November 25, 2006
Oscar Grant, 22, on January 1, 2009
Aaron Campbell, 25, on January 29, 2010
Aiyana Stanley-Jones, 7, on May 16, 2010
Alonzo Ashley, 29, on July 18, 2011
Trayvon Martin, 17, on February 26, 2012
Wendell Allen, 20, on March 7, 2012
Rekia Boyd, 22, on March 21, 2012
Jordan Davis, 17, on November 23, 2012
Jonathan Ferrell, 24, on September 14, 2013
Miriam Carey, 34, on October 3, 2013
Renisha McBride, 19, on November 2, 2013
Jordan Baker, 26, on January 16, 2014

Eric Garner, 43, on July 17, 2014

John Crawford III, 22, on August 5, 2014

Michael Brown, Jr., 18, on August 9, 2014

Laquan McDonald, 17, on October 20, 2014

Tamir Rice, 12, on November 22, 2014

Eric Harris, 44, on April 2, 2015

Walter Scott, 50, on April 4, 2015

Freddie Gray, 25, on April 19, 2015

Sandra Bland, 28, on July 13, 2015

Samuel DuBose, 43, on July 19, 2015

Alton Sterling, 37, on July 5, 2016

Philando Castile, 32, on July 6, 2016

Korryn Gaines, 23, on August 1, 2016

Terrence Crutcher, 40, on September 16, 2016

Keith Lamont Scott, 43, on September 20, 2016

Muhammad Muhayim, Jr., 43, on January 4, 2017

Jordan Edwards, 15, on April 29, 2017

Charleena Lyles, 30, on June 18, 2017

Stephon Clark, 22, on March 18, 2018

Antwon Rose II, 17, on June 19, 2018

Botham Jean, 26, on September 6, 2018

Javier Ambler, 40, on March 28, 2019

Pamela Turner, 44, on May 13, 2019

Josef Richardson, 38, July 25, 2019

Elijah McCain, 23, on August 30, 2019

Byron Williams, 50, on September 5, 2019

Atatiana Jefferson, 28, on October 12, 2019

Lionel Morris, 39, February 4, 2020

Ahmaud Arbery, 25, on February 23, 2020

Manuel Ellis, 33, on March 3, 2020
Breonna Taylor, 26, on March 13, 2020
Daniel T. Prude, 41, on March 23, 2020
Maurice Gordon, 28, on May 23, 2020
Dion Johnson, 28, on May 25, 2020
George Floyd, 46, on May 25, 2020
David McAtee, 53, on June 1, 2020
Rayshard Brooks, 27, on June 12, 2020
Julian Edward Roosevelt Lewis, 60, on August 7, 2020
Trayford Pellerin, 31, on August 21, 2020

Laws can confront the hate, but laws cannot convert the heart. Hate that existed in minds and souls back when still exists now. And even after all that Blacks have endured for over 400 years and because we see the hate that still exists, although we are tired, we cannot shut down. We cannot go silent or remain silent. And one of the best ways to make your voice heard is to vote. That is the least you can do; vote for those leaders who want to and who *will* break down walls, who insist on fairness for all, who believe that when one person grows and thrives, then we all grow and thrive.

We chose this day, **August 28, 2020**, to speak up and write this book because of this date's significance in Black history.

- On **August 28, 1955,** Emmett Till, a fourteen-year-old Black boy from Chicago, while visiting relatives in the South, is kidnapped, tortured, killed, wrapped with barbed wire, and thrown into the Tallahatchie River in Money, Mississippi, supposedly for whistling at Carolyn Bryant, a White woman. The facts leading to Till's death vary. Even after publicly confessing to his murder, Till's murderers are never found guilty.

- On **August 28, 1963,** Rev. Dr. Martin Luther King, Jr., minister and civil rights activist, stands in front of the Lincoln Memorial to deliver his "I Have a Dream" speech at the March on Washington, formally known as the March on Washington for Jobs and Freedom, or The Great March. It is held in Washington, DC with the purpose of advocating for civil and economic rights for Blacks.
- On **August 28, 2008,** then-Senator Barack H. Obama, II accepts the democratic nomination for president, becoming the first Black man ever to win the nomination and the first Black president of the United States of America.

Be Aware: Realize There Is So Much More to Us

We love this country, but sometimes it feels like it does not fully love us back. What we want—what we *need*—is for our history in this country to not be swept under the rug. What we need is to not feel as if we should be quiet and keep moving. What need is to not receive from others a sentiment of "Yes, that was horrible what happened to your ancestors. Now, get over it." What we need is to be seen, to be heard, to be supported, and we need everyone to have a heightened sense of awareness. And the fact you have this book in your hands speaks volumes.

First, realize systematic racism extends beyond how Blacks are treated by police. It exists in banking and lending practices, education, business, and just about every other aspect of life.

Next, focus on the youth; engage in teaching them to respect everyone, no matter how they look, and address racism in education. Children need to see books that include main characters of all shades, schools need to attract more Black (and Black male) teachers, and funding for schools predominantly attended by Blacks needs to be more equitable.

Next, speak up and support Blacks. Encourage resource groups for Black, indigenous, and people-of-color (BIPOC) colleagues, apply mentorship opportunities for them, recognize and cultivate their talents and strengths, and promote them.

Additionally, get involved. Whether it is political action; petitions; demonstrations; protests; social media engagement; or participating in Black Lives Matter, the NAACP, or the National Urban League, find your zone, and do something to make an impact.

Finally, continue to educate yourself so you can better understand your Black colleagues and their perspectives beyond what is offered in the media and what you see and read during the month of February. (Black History Month started with noted Black historian, scholar, educator, and publisher Carter G. Woodson, who started Negro History Week in 1926, which took place the second week of February. This month was chosen to coincide with the birthdays of Frederick Douglass, a leader in the abolitionist movement, author, and public speaker, who pushed for equality and human rights until his death in 1895, and Abraham Lincoln. In 1969, Carl Gregory and Dwayne White, Black educators and leaders of Black Students United at Kent State University, suggested devoting an entire month to celebrate the history of Blacks, and in 1970 the university celebrated its first Black History Month. On February 10, 1976, President Gerald Ford recognized Black History Month on a nationwide scale, stating "In the Bicentennial year of our Independence, we can review with admiration the impressive contributions of Black Americans to our national life and culture.")

Be aware that much greatness comes from us—more than what you see in the news and other media. To document this, here is a partial list, in alphabetical order by last name, of notable accomplishments and/or firsts by American Blacks:

Alvin Ailey utilized dance to the fight for justice and founded the Alvin Ailey American Dance Theatre.

Macon Allen was the first Black licensed to practice law.

Richard Allen founded the African Methodist Episcopal Church in 1794, the first independent denomination in the United States.

Harold Amos was the first Black department chair at Harvard Medical School.

Maya Angelou was a poet, memoirist, and civil rights activist, who was regarded as one of the first Black women able to publicly discuss her personal life, presenting a Black woman as the central character in literature, when her first book, *I Know Why the Caged Bird Sings*, was published in 1969.

Arthur Robert Ashe, Jr. was the first Black tennis player selected to the United States Davis Cup team and the only Black man to ever win the singles title at Wimbledon, the U.S. Open, and the Australian Open.

Benjamin Banneker, among other accomplishments, constructed a wooden clock, assisted in the survey of the original boundaries of the District of Columbia, and wrote a series of almanacs.

William Hames "Count" Basie was the first Black male Grammy award winner in 1958.

Patricia Bath invented the Laserphaco probe in 1986. Along with its methods of operation, the Laserphaco revolutionized cataract surgery. Bath was the first Black woman to receive a patent for a medical invention.

Guion Bluford was the first Black to go into space in 1983.

Jane Matilda Bolin, LL.B., was the first Black woman to serve as a judge in the United States in 1939. Prior to that, she was the first Black woman to graduate from Yale Law School, the first to join the New York City Bar Association, and the first to join the New York City Law Department.

Sarah Boone invented the ironing board.

Edward Bouchet was the first Black to earn a Ph.D., receiving a physics doctorate from Yale University in 1876.

Otis Boykin invented the artificial heart pacemaker control unit.

Marlin Briscoe, playing for the Broncos in 1968, was the first Black quarterback to start a pro football game.

Gwendolyn Brooks was the first Black to win the Pulitzer Prize for poetry on May 1, 1950.

Marie Van Brittan Brown and **Albert Brown** invented the home security system and patented the closed-circuit television security system in 1966.

Blanche Kelso Bruce was the first elected Black senator to serve a full term. (In 1870, **Hiram R. Revels**, also of Mississippi, was the first elected Black senator but did not complete a full term.)

Alexa Canady was the first Black female neurosurgeon.

George Carruthers patented the far-ultraviolet camera and spectrograph on November 11, 1969, which was used by the National Aeronautics and Space Administration (NASA) when it launched Apollo in 1972.

Ben Carson was the first surgeon to successfully separate craniopagus twins.

George Washington Carver, the most prominent Black scientist of the early twentieth century, discovered hundreds of uses for vegetables, fruits, and peanuts.

Charles W. Chappelle designed and invented the long-distance-flight airplane, which was displayed at the 1911 First Industrial Airplane Show in New York City.

Shirley Chisholm was the first Black congresswoman in 1968 and the first Black to make a bid for the U.S. presidency as a major-party candidate.

Kenneth Bancroft Clark was the first Black president of the American Psychological Association in 1966.

Bessie Coleman, in 1921, became the first Black (and person of Native American descent) to hold a pilot's license.

John William Coltrane was a jazz saxophonist, composer, and musical pioneer, who led at least fifty recording sessions, appeared on many albums by other musicians, and remains one of the most influential saxophonists in music history.

Misty Copeland, in 2015, became the first Black to be appointed as a principal dancer for American Ballet Theatre.

David Crosthwait, Jr. received more than forty patents relating to heating, ventilation, and air conditioning systems.

George Crum invented the potato chip on August 24, 1853.

Rebecca Davis Lee Crumpler was the first Black woman in 1864 to earn an M.D. in the United States.

Marie Maynard Daly was the first Black woman to earn a Ph.D. in chemistry.

Mark Dean co-invented the color IBM PC monitor and the gigahertz chip in the early 1980s and 1999, respectively.

James Derham was the first Black to formally practice medicine although he did not hold an M.D.

Charles Drew invented the blood bank in 1940.

Paul Laurence Dunbar was a poet, novelist, and playwright, who was one of the first Black American writers to establish an international reputation.

Sarah Jane Woodson Early was the first Black woman college instructor, teaching at Wilberforce College in 1858.

Edward Kennedy "Duke" Ellington, widely considered a pivotal figure in the history of jazz, was a composer, pianist, and leader of a jazz orchestra, which he led from 1923 until his death in 1974.

Robert F. Flemming, Jr. invented the "Euphonica" guitar in 1886.

Althea Gibson was the first Black to play in and win Wimbledon and the United States national tennis championship (U.S. Open) in 1956.

Sarah E. Goode invented the cabinet bed and was the first Black woman to receive a patent in the United States.

George F. Grant was the first Black professor at Harvard and invented the wooden golf tee.

Fannie Lou Hamer was a voting and women's rights activist, community organizer, and leader in the civil rights movement, who co-founded the Freedom Democratic Party and the National Women's Political Caucus and who organized Mississippi's Freedom Summer and the Student Nonviolent Coordinating Committee.

Lorraine Vivian Hansberry was the first Black female author to have a play performed on Broadway. At the age of 29, she was the first Black dramatist, the fifth woman, and the youngest playwright to win the New York Drama Critics' Circle Award.

Kamala D. Harris is the first Black and the first South Asian woman to accept a major party's vice presidential nomination.

James Mercer Langston Hughes is best known as a leader of the Harlem Renaissance, who wrote novels, short stories, plays, poetry, operas, essays, and works for children as well as two volumes of autobiography, *The Big Sea* and *I Wonder as I Wander*, and he translated several works of literature into English.

Zora Neale Hurston wrote four novels, with the most popular one being *Their Eyes Were Watching God*, published in 1937, and she wrote more than 50 short stories, plays, and essays.

Jesse Jackson was a 1984 and 1988 Democratic presidential nominee candidate and is the founder of Rainbow/PUSH, a nonprofit organization that pursues social justice, civil rights, and political activism.

Mary Jackson was NASA's first Black female engineer.

Mae Jemison became the first Black woman to go to space in 1992.

Thomas L. Jennings was the first Black granted a patent in the United States; it was for a dry cleaning process called dry scouring.

Jack Johnson was the first Black to become a heavyweight boxing champion in 1908 and had a winning streak until 1915.

James Weldon Johnson was a writer and civil rights activist, who was the NAACP's first Black executive secretary and who was known for his poems, novels, and anthologies during the Harlem Renaissance.

Lonnie Johnson holds more than 80 U.S. patents; worked on the stealth bomber project for the Air Force and the Galileo space probe for NASA; and invented the Super Soaker water gun toy, which was first patented in 1986.

Robert Johnson became the first Black billionaire in 2001 as the owner of Black Entertainment Television (BET).

Frederick McKinley Jones invented automatic refrigeration systems, receiving a patent on July 12, 1940. It's because of this invention that long-haul trucks, railroad cars, and ships can transport foods and other perishable items.

John Mercer Langston was, in 1855, the first Black male lawyer; one of the first Black elected officials in the country when elected as town clerk in Brownhelm Township, Ohio; the first dean of Howard University's law school; and the first president of what is now the historically black university, Virginia State University.

Lewis Latimer invented the carbon-filament light bulb, which was patented in January of 1881. While Thomas Edison created the first light bulb, it was Latimer who made the bulb cheaper to produce and more efficient so it could be used in everyday life.

John Legend is the first Black man to achieve EGOT status, wining Emmy, Grammy, Oscar, and Tony awards.

Mary Mahoney was the first Black to study and work as a professional nurse in the United States.

Thurgood Marshall was the first Black supreme court justice, serving from 1967 to 1991.

Hattie McDaniel was the first Black to win an academy award in 1940 for her role in *Gone With the Wind*.

Alexander Miles invented the automatically opening and closing electric elevator door.

Willie Hobbs Moore was the first Black woman to earn a Ph.D. in physics in 1972.

Garrett Augustus Morgan secured a patent for an improved sewing machine, and he invented the traffic signal in 1923, a hair-straightening product, and a respiratory device that provided the blueprint for the World War I gas mask.

Toni Morrison, born Chloe Ardelia Wofford, was a novelist, essayist, book editor, and college professor, who received national attention with *Song of Solomon*, published in 1977. She also won the **Pulitzer Prize** for *Beloved*. In 1993, she was awarded the Nobel Prize in Literature, gaining her worldwide recognition.

Mansa Musa, while he was not an American Black, he *was Black*, and it must be noted that he has been described as the wealthiest individual of the Middle Ages and perhaps, with indescribable wealth, the wealthiest of person all time. Musa was the tenth emperor of the Mali Empire, an Islamic West African state.

Barack H. Obama, II is the first Black president of the United States.

Jesse Owens was a four-time Olympic gold medalist at the 1936 Berlin Olympics, an accomplishment that had never been achieved by anyone up to that point in history. A year earlier, he set three world records and tied another, all in less than an hour at the 1935 Big Ten track meet in Ann Arbor, Michigan.

Sidney Poitier is the first Black man to win an Oscar in 1964 for Best Actor in *Lilies of the Field*. It would be nearly forty years later before another Black man would have such an honor, when **Denzel Washington** won an Oscar in 1990 for Best Supporting Actor in *Glory*.

Lucy Ann Stanton was the first Black woman to receive a four-year college degree, graduating from Oberlin College in 1850 and delivering the graduation address entitled "A Plea for The Oppressed." (Some sources cite **Mary Jane Patterson** as the first Black woman in the United States known to have earned a bachelor's degree, graduating from Oberlin College in 1862.)

Kwame Ture, born Stokely Standiford Churchill Carmichael, was a prominent organizer in the civil rights movement in the United States and the global Pan-African movement, and he developed the Black Power movement while leading the Student Nonviolent Coordinating Committee, and served as the "Honorary Prime Minister" of the Black Panther Party and as a leader of the All-African People's Revolutionary Party.

Alexander Lucius Twilight was the first Black college graduate, graduating from Middlebury College in 1823.

Madam C. J. Walker was the first female self-made millionaire.

Booker T. Washington was from the last generation of Black American leaders born into slavery and was an educator, author, orator, and adviser to multiple U.S. presidents.

Ida Bell Wells-Barnett was arguably the most famous Black woman in America. She was an investigative journalist, educator, and one of the NAACP founders.

James Edward Maceo West patented the electroacoustic transducer electret microphone in 1962. It is estimated that 90% of microphone designs today are based on West's original design.

Phillis Wheatley (also spelled Phyllis and Wheatly) was the first Black published author, writing a book of poetry.

Daniel Hale Williams was the first physician to perform a successful open-heart surgery in the United States in 1893 and founded the first nonsegregated hospital in the United States.

Peter Williams, Jr. was cofounder of the first Black-owned and -operated newspaper, *Freedom's Journal*.

Oprah Gail Winfrey, is best known for her talk show, *The Oprah Winfrey Show*, the highest-rated television program of its kind in history, running in syndication for a quarter of a century. She is the richest Black person of the twentieth century, is North America's first Black multibillionaire, and has been identified as the greatest Black philanthropist in American history.

Be aware of the trajectory of our experiences in America. Be aware that Black people carry with them a history that is unique to them. Be aware that for most of us, when you see our last names, you do not see the last names of our Black ancestors; in far too many instances, you see the last names of our ancestors' slave owners and the history attached to those names. Be aware that we view the world through a different lens. Be aware that when we step out of our homes each day, our reality is in stark contrast to our non-Black neighbors' realities in that we know there is always that looming possibility we will be treated based on how we look, rather than on who we are.

And, like countless other parents, we want our son to have a life experience that is not based on the color of his skin. For our son, we want him to be seen as a human being; that if he walks into a building to buy a car or if he attends school or shows up in any place, he is seen as being equal to any other person on the planet. As so many other mothers and fathers see their Black sons and daughters, for our son, we want him to be seen as we see him:

kind
gentle
intelligent
curious
lighthearted
easygoing
hilariously funny with an infectious smile
loving
helpful
sweet
friendly
playful
cheerful
active
bubbly
fun
handsome
quick on is feet—literally and figuratively
one with a sartorial style, even as early as the age of four

who is also a(n)…

lover of books and words

international traveler
solar system and extreme weather fanatic
student of the game of chess
metropolitan infrastructure enthusiast

and a beloved…

teammate
classmate
friend
cousin
nephew
grandson
son

who will grow up to be…

a most incredible, strong, bold Black man, who will be influential, who will perform great works, and who will make so many so proud.

Every Black person is not perfect.

Yes, some of us may have a different energy, a different spirit and zest, or a different approach to certain matters, but…

Every Black person is not to be feared. Every Black person is not violent. Every Black person is not angry or fiery.

Every Black man is not a threat. Every Black man is not out to harm their communities. And every Black man is not a criminal.

Black men are loved.

They *are* love.

They are strong.
They are wise.

They are valued.

They are powerful.

They are blessings.

Let them shine.

Let them live.

Let them breathe.

About Aaron and Bridgett

Aaron and Bridgett are native Texans who met in northwest Houston the day after Thanksgiving 2002; married in southeast Texas on July 1, 2006; and lived in Cypress, Texas, before relocating to the Phoenix, Arizona, area the day before Thanksgiving 2009. Proud graduates of HBCUs Texas Southern University in Houston, Texas, and Prairie View A&M University in Prairie View, Texas, respectively, Aaron and Bridgett keep each other laughing on a daily basis, love love love traveling, and have more fun together and with their son than words can adequately articulate.

MY ONLY REGRET IS THERE WERE NO CAMERAS
Travis Hardin

It is humbling to be Black in America. With the ability to capture footage of a few hundred years' challenge, the world is now getting a glimpse of what being Black has looked like. So many people are saying how times are getting worse with the images and videos being shown across various platforms. The reality is, things are not getting worse, they are simply being caught on camera.

I think back to my teenage years when my father would constantly remind me, prior to obtaining my driver's permit and my driver's license, the dos and don'ts if and when I was ever pulled over by the police. I remember thinking, *"Why would I need to follow these steps, depending on the scenario?"*

There were things I would do if I was pulled over in the daytime, at nighttime, and if there was one officer or multiple officers. There were certain things I would say if someone was with me, if there was a female in the car, or if there were people of a different color riding with me. I had to know where to position my hands and to remain still without making any sudden movements as officers approached my vehicle. All these things as a fifteen-year-old, trying to just receive my permit, on many occasions, made me think that I didn't care to drive that bad.

But I wanted to have my independence to drive and travel. I quickly learned the constant reminders and test runs as my father would sit in the passenger seat, asking me certain questions. I was pulled over and allowed to drive off a few times, while using the training my father taught me. It was one night as a college sophomore that proved my father's training was so invaluable.

I entered Portland en route to Grand Rapids, Michigan, on a Saturday night when blue and red lights flashed in my rearview mirror. I knew I was not speeding because I was on cruise control, listening to Brian McKnight and eating Funyuns. The single car approached my vehicle on the side of the road of I-96. It was dark, so I rolled the window down, turned the interior lights on and placed my hands on the door, just enough outside the window where officers could see my hands.

Two officers approached my vehicle and immediately told me to get out of the car. I did as requested, per my father's training. I politely asked why I was being pulled over and was told "Niggers don't ask questions, they listen." As a nineteen-year-old, I was ready to yell something back, but I had rehearsed time and time again with my father, so I was able to remain calm.

I was told to get on the ground, and they opened all four doors to my Saturn and opened the trunk. I had my college baseball bag in there, as I was a college athlete and always had my equipment with me. They yelled and said, "We know you ain't no college ballplayer because niggers don't go to college and they don't play base-ball." I remained quiet. I prayed.

By now, three additional cars pulled up, and there was a total of six officers standing around me shouting racial slurs. I did happen to have my college identification on me and said I could prove that I was in college and played baseball. I gave the coach's name and one of the officers knew the coach. He quickly said to the officers to let me up and told me to get in my car and leave. I think back to that night. What if I didn't have my identification? What if I had not mentioned Coach Bo?

My only regret is there were no cameras.

What needs to change, and why is it so important for change to happen sooner than later?

Humility among all humanity. Humility moves us from the center to the side. What we are going to be should come before what we see. What are we going to do today that will set us up for who we will become? We must humble ourselves to effectively get through our current challenges. When we humble ourselves, we remove ourselves from the center of everything and realize that we do not have all the answers. We realize we are not as good as we thought we were, and we recognize that titles at the beginning or the end of my name don't do a thing for me. We learn that the possessions we have do not mean a thing.

Humility is a wonderful virtue that moves me out of the way in order for me to put other's needs in front of my own. It allows me to be concerned about other's wants and desires. It allows me to grieve when others grieve, smile when they smile, and celebrate when they celebrate.

It is important that we, as humankind, grow in the area of adjusting to make it through and to be better on the other side. One way to get through a crisis is making adjustments. The best way to make adjustments is to humble ourselves. Things that we did a few weeks or months ago will no longer work. The road so frequently traveled and comfortable has now come to a dead end. We all must be humble enough to remove the focus from *I* or *me* and put the focus on *us*.

College coaches would work on our baseball swings for hours while other coaches worked with pitchers and catchers for hours every single day. They would always tell us that the team who made the adjustments with the least amount of resistance during games was the team that would more often win. I think of that today, as we struggle through our current state as humans. Humankind will win, as long as we humble ourselves enough to make the necessary adjustments in order for everyone to win.

How can we learn more?

One of my favorite books and a place I believe we can gain much of the momentum needed to be victorious during this time in our history is *Improving Your Serve: The Art of Unselfish Living* by Charles R. Swindoll. It provides practical steps to move from selfishness to selflessness. We can all gain more if we all give more.

Biography

Travis Hardin, internationally acclaimed speaker, trainer, and mentor, knows the power of belief. A Tennessee native, he received his Bachelor of Arts from Aquinas College (Grand Rapids, Michigan) in 1999. As a John Maxwell certified speaker and trainer, he is equipped in aiding personal and professional growth through study and practical application of proven leadership methods.

For more than twenty years, Travis has given inspirational speeches for purposeful living, specifically on production capacity, personal and professional growth, overcoming disciplinary challenges, and diversity and inclusion. His self-reflective transparency in speeches and workshops has provided him with opportunities to speak around the globe.

As a community advocate, Travis was honored as a top 100 candidate for the John C. Maxwell Transformational Leadership Award, Wells Fargo Diversity and Inclusion Champion Award, Toastmasters International Distinguished Toastmaster Award, and United Way Worldwide nominee for a reality series telling the story of ordinary people making extraordinary differences in their communities.

It gives Travis the greatest level of humility to inspire people and demonstrate in practice that all individuals can grow and increase their positive influence on this generation and those around them beyond their wildest expectations. He challenges people to a new season of growth that begins with their passion to reach new levels. Travis lives in Phoenix, Arizona, with his wife and daughter.

SILENCE IS VIOLENCE
Dr. James Smith, Jr., CSP

My mother was my first navigator. Rebecca Nanci Smith could deliver a lesson. The lessons I learned at her feet steer my life to this day. Growing up, like many ambitious kids with dreams of a great future, I, unfortunately, wanted to do everything my way. Initially, her lessons weren't cemented into my mind until I was in the throes of the struggle. That's where her words of wisdom resonated the most.

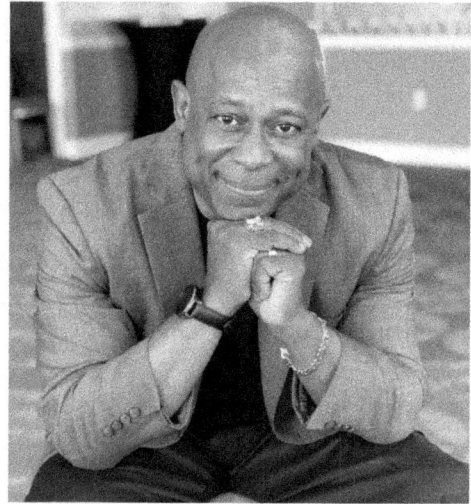

I can still hear her.

- Jimmy, work twice as hard as everyone else.
- Sit in the front row of every classroom.
- Smile for every identification photo that you take (library card, driver's license, membership card—you'll never know when that smile will be a saving grace).
- Never give others bullets (reasons) to shoot you because they already have guns.
- Education is your secret weapon.

These are messages that I cling to and are my life guidance system today.

I remember in my twenties reading Ralph Wiley's book, *Why Black People Tend to Shout: Cold Facts and Wry Views from a Black Man's World.* That book put my life into perspective and in high definition, even at that early age. Now, as a fifty-nine-year-old, I'm still shouting, but I've also lived a life of praying, crying, reaching, struggling, celebrating, not understanding, achieving, and shaking my head. Realizing that I live in a world that professes to want equality for all but has institutionalized systems in place to negate that possibility is extremely disconcerting. Nevertheless, that *is* my reality, and I continue to persevere.

Being Black in America today is arduous yet edifying. It means being personally accountable and responsible for your todays and your tomorrows—knowing that you're going to consistently have to bring value to nearly every situation. It means having to be as authentic as you can. I learned long ago that "going along to get along" and "faking it until you make it" were not the tools of champions. You have to let people know where you stand. I also learned that silence is violence; you have to speak truth to power.

Being Black in America today is fighting racist and oppressive mindsets that attempt to undermine your success. Twisted mindsets that say when minorities fail, they fail as a group and when they succeed, they succeed as individuals; and that when white people fail, they fail as individuals and they succeed as a group.

Being Black in America today is a constant reminder that leaders are readers and that you have to do your research and truly understand what's happening around you if you want change. Being Black in America means daily confronting white privilege, hate, institutionalized racism, bias, microinequities, and microaggressions.

Even today, I am often the only Black person in the room or on the team. I think, *Here I go, being Jackie Robinson again.* I have to admit, however, those situations have certainly made me stronger and reinforced the idea that I have to continue to push forward and continue to be a part of the racial equality solution.

Being Black in America today means being resilient and not comparing yourself to your white counterparts. Moreover, being Black in America today means not colluding nor remaining the same; neither are options for professional or personal success.

Finally, being Black in America today is realizing that many white people don't understand or care about what it means to be Black in America today. And I get that! There are certainly moments when white people do care, however, I'd rather see those moments evolve into movements that reinforce their care.

Notwithstanding, being Black in America today keeps me sharp, proud, and focused, still working to create an environment where my children's tomorrows are much better than my todays.

What needs to change, and why is it so important for change to happen sooner than later?

Michael Vick served 548 days in the US Penitentiary, Leavenworth, a federal prison in Kansas, for running a dog-fighting operation in 2007. I remember it clearly. The former National Football League (NFL) quarterback and his Bad Newz Kennels tragedy made national news. The complexity of this saga, his arrest, and the lengthy sentence revealed a deep racial divide as stark as black and white—no dimensions of gray.

Many white communities seethed while many Black communities understood the phenomenon and systemic problem of over-policing and over-sentencing Black citizens. White Americans were in an uproar when, upon his release, Vick attempted (successfully) to make a comeback and resume his professional football career. The anger and frustration were real. White Americans condemned Vick for killing dogs. Black Americans, for years, have been frustrated for institutionalized racist systems that normalize the killing and incarceration of Black people at will.

A demand for racial and social justice now confronts the United States with a timely opportunity. Eight minutes and forty-six seconds reinforced this imperative. The COVID-19 pandemic created captive, quarantined audiences to watch the unfathomable George Floyd murder; it sent protestors to the streets and mourners to their knees.

What made this untimely and senseless killing different (from the other Black people who have met a similar fate of late) for me was that I sensed that many white Americans felt pain too. A number of my white friends and colleagues reached out to me to provide support and encouragement and to see how they could help.

Unfortunately, their outreach lasted two weeks. Afterward, there seemed to be a return to business as usual. Not for me! As a Black man, I am forever reminded, forever changed. Life or death can slip away in minutes at the hands of a system of hate. Therefore, I cannot be silent. My life is a protest, and I cannot quit!

For this racially, inequitable system to change, we must all sound our outrage—Black, white, brown, red, and all Americans. We must all demand change with our voices and actions. White Americans have their work to do. Opportunities will continue to confront them to use their privilege and power to move change in the right direction. Other groups have fought for justice for years. Inequality rules and the landscape appears to be getting worse.

What needs to change?

1. Actions
2. Behaviors
3. Mindsets
4. Belief systems
5. White privilege
6. Police brutality
7. Institutionalized racism

I remember watching former Riceville, Iowa, third-grade schoolteacher and now civil rights activist Jane Elliott present to a group of professionals circa1990. She asked the white participants to stand. She then said if they wanted to be treated the way the country treats Blacks, women, and other minority groups to remain standing. Everyone sat down. She finished by stating that if they know these groups are being treated unfairly, then why aren't they doing anything about it? As Elliott said, "If it [judging people based on skin color] can be learned, it can be unlearned" (Karina Bland, "Blue Eyes, Brown Eyes: What Jane Elliott's Famous Experiment Says about Race Fifty Years On," *The Republic*, November 17, 2017).

How can we learn more?

Resources

James John and Margaret Goff, "Anti-Black Racism: Where We Were, and Where We Are Today," *Urban Institute*, August 14, 2016.

Maja Hazell, "The Crippling Impact of Anti-Black Racism, and How Allies Can Act Against It." *Law.com*, June 18, 2020.

Nikita Stewart, "We Are Committing Educational Malpractice: Why Slavery is Mistaught—and Worse—in American Schools," *The New York Times Magazine*, August 19, 2019.

Books

How to Be an Antiracist by Ibram X. Kendi

Stamped from the Beginning: The Definitive History of Racist Ideas in America by
    Ibram X. Kendi

The Color of Law: A Forgotten History of How Our Government Segregated America by
    Richard Rothstein

White Fragility: Why It's So Hard for White People to Talk about Racism by Robin
    DiAngelo

Biography

James Smith, Jr. (certified speaking professional, president and chief executive officer of James Smith Jr. International) passionately works with audiences providing high-performance solutions and breakthroughs in the areas of leadership, authenticity, diversity and inclusion, organizational behavior, presentation and facilitation skills, and personal empowerment.

A sought-after speaker, coach, and educator, his workshops, keynotes, and executive coaching experiences have taken him to forty-three states and more than twenty-five countries in front of audiences of all sizes. Moreover, the personal power expert and author has worked with executives, leaders, and managers, coaching them in effective communication skills, employee development, and team synergy. In addition, he has coached speakers, trainers, and television and radio personalities in how to use storytelling to create memorable, engaging, and retention-based presentations.

Smith is an adjunct faculty member for Rutgers University MBA, Executive MBA, and International Executive MBA programs and for the Temple University Fox School of Business. In November 2008, he was featured on the cover of the National

Speakers Association *Speaker* magazine. His book, *The No Excuse Guide to Success: No Matter What Your Boss or Life Throws at You*, was nominated for a National Association for the Advancement of Colored People (NAACP) Image Award. In 2016, he received the coveted certified speaking professional (CSP) designation from the National Speakers Association (a designation that only 12 percent of the speakers in the world have).

Smith obtained his Bachelor of Arts in English degree from Widener University, his master's in journalism degree from Temple University, and his executive Doctor of Business Administration degree from Temple University Fox School of Business. Prior to forming James Smith Jr. International, he held leadership and consulting roles for The Bob Pike Group, Simmons Associates, CoreStates Bank, The Vanguard Group, and the Prudential Insurance Company of America.

Smith's focus is on personal power, growth, and authenticity to create a mindset shift in learners and audience members. He wants people to take 100 percent responsibility and accountability for their behaviors, actions, and results and to jump into their *bigness*. This will help them reach unprecedented levels of performance, authenticity, and transparency.

Smith has authored three books. *From Average to Awesome: Lessons for Living an Extraordinary Life, Crash and Learn: 600+ Road-Tested Tips to Keep Audiences Fired Up and Engaged!* and *The No Excuse Guide to Success: No Matter What Your Boss or Life Throws at You*. He coauthored *The Masters of Success* with Ken Blanchard, Mike Van Hoozer, Jack Canfield, John Christensen, and twelve other experts). He has also penned book chapters and articles for a number of publications.

Smith writes a weekly blog, "Jim's Journal," that reaches audiences all over the world. He facilitates two weekly Zoom webcasts—"The Dr. Jim Show" and

"Fearless Authenticity." When not *jimpact*ing, he spends his time working with organizations and individuals whose purpose is helping those on the autism spectrum and serving on the board of Variety, the Children's Charity in Philadelphia.

HEAR OUR POSITION TO UNDERSTAND OUR PAIN
Rachael Boone

Growing up in a small rural, segregated town, I remember the first time I realized I was Black. It was summertime, circa 1984, and I was working for my grandfather. I recall pushing that lawnmower up a hill on a hot scorching summer day. It had to be about ninety degrees or more. Sun was beaming on my face, so I stopped for a break and grabbed my water to quench my thirst. Shortly after that, I remember having to use the bathroom.

So, I took my eight-year-old self to the door of my grandfather's client. Mind you, he always liked handling the client while we worked. He would approach the door by ringing the doorbell of his client. He was always professional while speaking with the client, and his grandchildren would do the work. In today's world, he would have been considered business development, and we were his account managers.

On that particular day, my grandfather ran off to take care of another client. So, I walked up to the door as my grandfather usually did and rang the doorbell. This little old petite white lady in her late seventies came to the door. I proceeded by asking if I could use her bathroom, and she replied, "I don't allow coloreds to use my bathroom."

At that point, I realized I was different but didn't think twice about it, and I knew I had to use the bathroom. So, I took myself down the street to use the bathroom. I told my grandfather what happened. We continued to service the yard, but I was replaced with another cousin. I was removed from maintaining her yard.

That moment taught me a lot. That's the first time I realized that color matters. Even though we lived in a segregated town, my grandfather exposed us to a work ethic, relationship building, and business development with people who didn't look like us. He taught us how to conduct ourselves, which has helped me on my career journey, but I always knew that race mattered and played a factor in my life.

As a Black woman, mother, and human resources (HR) professional, I've seen microaggressions and racism play out. This has caused me a lot financially in my career along with the loss of promotions. I have zero tolerance for injustices and elitism. I've had colleagues say to me, "I don't consider you one of them . . . You're white/Black . . . I trust you . . . How did you get in with the good ole boys?" I've also been around Black people who have said to me, "I will only hire white people."

When confronted by those statements, I found myself in hot water because my reply would make my audience think about what they just said or asked me. Let me be clear, I don't stand for injustice at all. I'm so glad we are having these conversations because I can think back to 2013 when I worked for a company that bragged about having white male leaders, whose average age was forty-two. I remember being asked by my HR coworker if, because I was the only African American, I felt uncomfortable. I replied, "No, do you?"

Again, I'm so thankful we are having these conversations. For me, it's like a breath of fresh air because it shouldn't have taken the loss of lives to realize we want to feel like we belong, that our talents and voices matters. However, the deaths of George Floyd and Ahmaud Arbery woke up America in a way that I've never seen before.

As a mother, I've always made sure my son was exposed to opportunities and had friends from all walks of life. He is now a twenty-five-year-old man who has seen the videos, along with me, replaying over and over. It deepens the wounds. It made us upset. The clip from Ahmaud Arbery's murder, seeing him chased down in the streets by hunters. Racist hunters, who wanted to hunt Black people because of their fears and their right to do so. I immediately thought of myself, my son, running through adjacent neighborhoods on any typical day.

My hurt ached for Arbery's mom and his family. His killers hunted him like he was an animal in the wilderness. He was somebody's son, a future father. I was speechless, only to be followed by the death of George Floyd. When does it stop? As a mom, I feared for my son. This was one more thing I needed to add to our talk or preventive list to avoid any run-ins with ignorance and bigotry.

Being Black in corporate America and being a mom to a Black son, I always have to be on-guard. We are overly traumatized and overtaxed.

What needs to change, and why is it so important for change to happen sooner than later?

For me, what needs to change is getting involved in the community and for us as a community to value one another's lives. We need to learn our history and understand the power we have as a collective people. When we know our value, we will not accept less than or tolerate injustice.

How can we learn more?

People can learn more by listening to our stories. Hear our position to understand our pain. I don't believe in excuses. Because you're Black, it should not limit you but excite you!

I recommend watching the 2016 documentary *13th,* directed by Ava DuVernay. I recommend reading Michelle Alexander's *The New Jim Crow: Mass Incarceration in the Age of Colorblindness* and "The 1619 Project" essays by *The New York Times Magazine.*

Biography

Rachael Boone is the chief executive officer (CEO) and founder of BeEvolved HR, a human resources and leadership coaching consultancy organization based in Raleigh, North Carolina. She has created a movement about the evolution of women called SheEvolved, which has manifested itself in a conference series, workshops, and a forthcoming book.

Boone has over twenty years of expertise in both private and nonprofit organizations as a respected consultant in all areas of human resources management, corporate compliance, executive coaching, diversity, and quality management outcomes for staff and company growth and development.

Boone also serves as a resource for the United Nations Entity for Gender Equality and the Empowerment of Women (UN Women), an organization dedicated to gender equality and the empowerment of women. A global champion for women and girls, UN Women was established to accelerate progress on meeting their needs worldwide. Boone organizes Pink Slip Parties, which are catered to individuals who have been affected by downsizing and layoffs and brings together HR professionals in conferences. She also serves as a Triangle Advisor Committee Member for St. Jude Children's Research Hospital in Raleigh, North Carolina.

RACISM IS EXHAUSTING
Ranada Samuel

For me, being Black in America is great; racism is exhausting. It's necessary to distinguish the difference between the two (Imani Perry, "Racism Is Terrible. Blackness Is Not," *The Atlantic,* June 15, 2020). The obstacles, issues, and challenges I experience because of racism are evident in my professional and personal life.

Before I share, let's take a moment to ensure we are approaching the conversation from a mutual understanding. Life is hard, adulting is hard, home ownership is hard, and parenting is hard. There are few things in life that are easy, and I am not looking for a simple way out. My frustration is the added layer that the challenge of being Black adds to basic life functioning.

As a Black professional, research has shown that I'm likely to be offered less in salary than white professionals and have less likelihood to obtain a position in the C-Suite or board of directors for a Fortune 500 company (Heather Long and Andrew Van Dam, "The Black-White Economic Divide Is as Wide as It Was in 1968," *The Washington Post,* June 4, 2020) ("Women and Minorities on Fortune 500 Boards: More Room to Grow," *The Wall Street Journal,* March 12, 2019).

Racism from my professional life influences racism in my personal life in many ways, namely my housing options, which are based on my income. There are direct correlations between the amount of income I earn and the housing options and neighborhoods I select. I'm a parent also; the community I reside in influences the education options for my child. Will I be selecting the best public or charter school for my child, or will I be selecting the best private school education that I can afford within a reasonable daily commute for my child and me?

Racism is exhausting. Even in instances of travel, vacation, and leisure activities, racism is still there. Road trips are extremely dangerous, not just because of the obvious dangers associated with travel but because my spouse is a Black male (AJ Willingham, "Researchers Studied Nearly 100 Million Traffic Stops and Found Black Motorists Are More Likely to Be Pulled Over" CNN.com, March 21, 2019). But, what about nixing the road trip or trying a different type of adventure that might not be traditionally seen as a vacation option for Blacks like camping (including use of recreational vehicles), hiking, skiing, or mountain climbing? The looks, the whispers, and the tension when eye contact is made. Is it worth it? This is my vacation; racism is exhausting.

Keep in mind, we have not discussed professional qualifications and experience, education, and certifications or professional contributions to my employer. Some might say to try your hand as an entrepreneur to mitigate racism. Research also reveals that Black entrepreneurs experience additional hardships obtaining capital (Gene Marks, "Black-Owned Firms Are Twice as Likely to Be Rejected for Loans. Is This Discrimination?" *The Guardian*, January 16, 2020). Although being Black in America is great, racism continues to be exhausting because it has the potential to be at every encounter in my life.

What needs to change, and why is it so important for change to happen sooner than later?

It is time that we become the America that we envisioned ourselves to be but have never obtained. Langston Hughes articulates this well in the poem "Let America Be America Again."

We need to work collectively as a nation to dismantle systemic racism in government, corporations, communities, and neighborhoods. This will require a top-down and bottom-up approach to have lasting effects. Behind every policy, law, and procedure are people.

We need people to stand up and do the right thing because it is the right thing to do. If you are unsure of what the right thing is, *ask* someone and do your best until you find the right thing. Start by asking people how they would like to be treated and take action based on that.

Evaluate your current actions as a professional and community member. What are you actively doing to stop the advancement of systemic racism in your places of influence? In what ways have you exposed yourself to the opportunities to engage Blacks in professional and personal settings?

Join a professional organization within your industry for a year; fully engage and participate in events and conferences. There are several organizations to choose from in every industry, including the National Black MBA Association, the Association of Black Psychologists, and the African American Marketing Association, to name a few.

Consider joining a social group within your desired interest that has a Black chapter, such as Black Triathletes Association, The Yarn Mission, and United Black Golfers Association. Whatever your interest is, it is likely to have a Black chapter.

In short, make a commitment to be the change you want to see. Get comfortable being uncomfortable, and try your best to diversify your places of influence. This change needs to happen now, and it needs to start with individuals. We must be purposefully people of diversity, equity, and inclusion. We can no longer wait and expect someone else to do it. We are the people who need to do it now.

How can we learn more?

There is a plethora of resources available to expand awareness and knowledge concerning racial injustice, along with recommended action steps to take. The first step starts with making a commitment to do something and then do it. One of the most important actions is to take time to do self-reflections concerning your emotions and actions when you observe racism, benefit from racism, and/or engage in racist behavior. Take time to reflect on the situation and ask yourself how and why you reached this state.

Consider speaking to a professional counselor, psychologist, or psychiatrist about your feelings. Take it a step further and have the same conversations with Black professional counselors, Black psychologists, and Black psychiatrists. Push yourself outside your comfort zone and challenge yourself in the areas that are most uncomfortable.

To have lasting change, we must be the change we want to see in our areas of influence. This link contains a list of antiracism resources: https://bit.ly/2NHhqk6. Let this be a starting place on your personal journey to inclusion.

Biography

Ranada Samuel, a human resources professional, specializes in results through relationship building. She supports companies in building employment branding campaigns to attract top talent. To nurture this relationship, she assists in the development of talent acquisition networks (TAN) to keep potential applicants and employers engaged in information sharing. By assisting companies with the development of TAN, it provides a great advantage in the recruitment process, ensuring that top talent quickly fills positions. It's not just about hiring top talents, it's about keeping them.

Through stellar training and development, Samuel establishes long-lasting relationships. She is actively involved in training and developing employees. She has hands-on experience developing specialized course designs, working with diverse populations, including adult learners, e-learning, and team train-the-trainer facilitation. Organizations might replicate processes, materials, and structures of other successful organizations, but the employees distinguish it from competitors.

Samuel's passion to contribute to the professional development of others and to leave a legacy of excellence is what drives her to ensure success on every project. Her patience and flexibility allow her to successfully interact with people of widely differing levels of experience, intelligence, emotional intelligence, education, knowledge, skills, and abilities, which enhance her capacity to effectively manage an organization's employees.

Samuel serves as the voice of management to employees and as an advocate for employees to management. As a supporter of both the business and the people's perspectives, she exhibits diplomacy in every situation and is committed to training and developing professionals so they can exceed expectations while adding to the organization's profitability. She is ready for the next challenge that will allow her to effectively contribute to business viability and success through the strategic management of human capital.

WHERE IS THE BASIC CONCERN FOR HUMAN LIFE?
Alfred Gleason, Jr.

It seems to be difficult to describe being Black in America in a way that is easy to understand for those who aren't Black or have had a similar experience. Being Black in America many times feels like being in something like Gary Ross's 2012 film *The Hunger Games* but being gaslighted and told that you are not. In the story, there is a great divide between the wealthy and the poor. The wealthy restrict sustenance to oppress the poor inhabitants.

In our country, the foundation of the wealth was built on the backs of our ancestors in slavery, which created the great divide between the rich and the poor. Once slaves were freed, they had to start with nothing and were forced to live in poverty. Getting out of poverty was a serious challenge because sustenance was withheld from them.

There has always been a subset of rules and laws that prevented us from living the American dream, even though we also fought for that dream as a people. Blacks have been further oppressed by being denied the right to vote; being forced to have an inferior education; and having to contend with discrimination that is consistently ingrained in the minds of everyone in society by the derogatory images, videos, and language that are shown in the media.

In *The Hunger Games,* the tessera (voluntary food rationing) is a selection system for the "battle to the death" game. If individuals were selected, they were ripped from their families and sent to an almost sure death. It reminds me of how the police disproportionately search within our communities looking for who they can send to jail, separating Black people from their families. Some individuals choose to do illegal things, while others feel forced to, in an effort to survive. In both cases, they increase their chances of being selected and being sentenced to "death." Jail is not necessarily death, but imprisonment is the death of life as most of us know it, losing the right to vote and the ability to get a regular job ever again.

The wealthy in *The Hunger Games* have little regard for the life of the poor, like the disregard we see shown to Black people in America. Watching the men in the recorded killings of George Floyd, Ahmaud Arbery, Rayshard Brooks, and many other recent examples are evidence and proof of this lack of regard for the life of Black people.

The police acted with audacity and demonstrated a lack of concern for repercussions. How else could an officer kneel on a man's neck for eight minutes and forty-six seconds and ignore his cries for help, all while being filmed?! In Rayshard Brooks's case, the police opened fire on an inebriated man running away from them, in a busy fast-food restaurant parking lot. Where is the basic concern for human life?

Many White people act like the elite in the movie. They might not have seen the injustice firsthand, but they willingly turn a blind eye to what's going on or choose to stay ignorant of what's going on, despite the outcry of the oppressed.

As a Black man speaking about this, people have attempted to make me feel like I was crazy, stuck in the past, or even a bigot or racist. There are those who survive the games and make it out, but it is a relatively small number. There are times when class supersedes race, and those Black people who enjoy that privilege might have a different experience; but it doesn't mitigate those who live it every day. Many Black folks go through the experience of doubting what they know happened to them or question their actions, wondering if they did something to deserve the unjust treatment.

What needs to change, and why is it so important for change to happen sooner than later?

The necessary change is not easy, but it is simple. The foundation of our nation is the family. For things to change, we must begin there. History has shown us that morality can't be legislated, but parents have the most important impact on children, especially at a young age. Parents, particularly those who are racist, and those who are indifferent, need to stop teaching their kids to be the same—not only verbally, but through their actions. This is the long-term solution that can eradicate racism in this country.

Because racism is systematic, many established systems that support it need to be revamped or changed completely. This includes changing policing, media, and education for starters.

Policing needs to change by eliminating the targeting of neighborhoods of color, removing incentives (like guns and money) for police forces based on drug busts in those same communities, and more accountability for the treatment of suspects when they are apprehended.

For the **media**, there needs to be accountability for how the stories are reported. Watch most any broadcast to see that accurate and unbiased reporting has taken a back seat, as the focus is on the dramatic because it helps sell advertisements. When reporters are caught making an error, a retraction is placed in the least conspicuous spot, if it's mentioned at all.

The media consistently portray Blacks and minorities in a negative light, from showing the worst picture or video of a news story subject to interviewing the worst-looking or sounding eyewitness on the scene. Terms like "thug" describe Black men, regardless of their position or character. For example, former President Barack Obama was called a "political thug." National Football League (NFL) player Richard Sherman was called a thug for expressing his feelings. Both individuals are articulate Black men who graduated from prestigious universities that most people in the country could not qualify to get into. They have exemplary records as great citizens and nothing to justify calling them thugs.

The **education** system is also a part of the problem. Blacks are generally left out of history, except during Black History Month, and many of our contributions to this country are ignored or downplayed. Slavery, when covered, is pictured in a much better light than what happened. The people who our country holds in high esteem, and many of our traditions and customs, have horrible roots and our schools continue to uphold them as heroes above reproach.

Denial of proper and equal education, adequate funding, and school administration all need to be improved. Along with the other areas I mentioned, the problems are deeply and strategically intertwined in the fabric of our schools and society and must be intentionally removed for things to change.

How can we learn more?

One of the biggest problems is willful ignorance. For those who want to understand and be a part of the solution, I recommend watching the Jane Elliott videos on her "Blue Eyes/Brown Eyes Exercise" and reading a book called *The New Jim Crow: Mass Incarceration in the Age of Colorblindness* by Michelle Alexander. Both provide great insight to the problems we face and point to what things need to be changed.

Biography

Alfred Gleason, Jr. is the chief executive officer (CEO) of Curator of Nonsense and loves helping people by making the complex simple. He is passionate about bringing awareness and understanding to information and concepts that can fuel success. With over twenty years of experience teaching leadership and soft skills in some capacity, Gleason is committed to sharing what he can to see others flourish. He is a published writer, author, and speaker who enjoys using creativity and innovation across multiple platforms. He has produced content on myriad topics, including peak performance, leadership, soft skills, confidence, relationships, and luxury living.

Gleason has a bachelor's degree in business from Morehouse College, a Master of Business Administration, and is currently a doctoral student studying performance psychology at Grand Canyon University. He has coached and consulted professionals in business, sports, and entertainment.

Gleason is a roller coaster enthusiast who enjoys traveling, reading, and coaching youth sports. He resides in Gilbert, Arizona, with his wife Alina, and has the joy of being a father to Antoinea; Aubree; Amani; Al, III; Amari; Aulani; and Alani.

MY HEART FELT HEAVY AND MY HANDS FELT HELPLESS
Inacent Saunders

I struggled long and hard about how to respond to the question, "What is it like to be Black in America?" Many, much more eloquent writers—some of the greatest to put pen to paper for novels, speeches, songs, essays, and poems—have expressed their feelings with greater effect than I think I ever could.

I grasped at the words of Ntozake Shange, James Baldwin, W. E. B. Du Bois, Toni Morrison, and others for inspiration. But I quickly realized that although their words often resonated with me, none of them got to the heart of the matter. No, that's not it. I should state none of them captured *my* heart on the matter. Although I could answer this question with a "collective response"—a well-known one from one of these great writers that would illicit many head nods due to its familiarity amongst Blacks in America—this response, my response, needs not seek the words of another. I need to do the work, the soul-searching work, to make sure my response flows from my own heart, my own soul. Anything else would be inauthentic.

If the year 2020 has taught me anything so far, it's that I need to stop shrinking back. Instead, I need to let my light shine, authentically. Especially as one who has felt muted in recent years. Me, a lover of the written word, one who appreciates great discourse on difficult topics . . . me.

I've been too afraid to say, to even write, what I was feeling. Why? Because it was painful, and I didn't want to feel the pain. Because it was hard to articulate, with any tact, what I was thinking. But let's face it, when one is in pain, tact should be the last thing on his or her mind, right? You don't expect bruised animals *not* to howl with every bit of pain they're feeling. But for me, for meek, humble, level-headed me, tact was important. When I couldn't express myself with any real composure, I stopped trying to express myself at all. I stopped writing. I stopped speaking. I stopped engaging in any conversations about what it means to Black in America.

Four years ago, I entered into what I call "the numb years" in my life . . . the years in which I decided I needed to shut it all down. No more anger. No more outrage. No more sadness. I'll share more about that in a bit. But here we are. Here I am, breaking my silence with this collaborative *A Collective Breath* project because it's time.

The year 2020 came and showed me that I could no longer be silent. I don't need to say anything profound, nothing life-changing. But I could no longer afford to just be quiet. As one of my favorite authors, Zora Neale Hurston, once wrote, "There are years that ask questions and years that answer" (*Their Eyes Were Watching God*). After four years of silence, that asked many questions, 2020 is here to answer.

The numb years . . . If I had to think back to how they even came about, how I reached my breaking point, I would go back to July 2014, when the rest of the world and I watched a viral video of Eric Garner die as a result of an illegal chokehold by a member of the New York City Police Department.

There had been other instances of excessive force used by police officers caught on tape and shared online. As a 1980s baby, I still vividly remember the beating of Rodney King by members of the Los Angeles Police Department that was caught on tape and shared on the news, night after night, for the world to see.

But the Eric Garner recording struck me differently. Maybe it was because of my age. My sense of mortality and vulnerability only increases as I get older. Perhaps it was because it was in New York City, the only place I had ever called home up until that point. Perhaps it was because Eric represented the brothers I knew who routinely stood in front of the corner store, a common meeting place, without any truly malicious intent. The brothers who made me feel safer than I would had they not been standing there, simply because they were the familiar faces that waved and exchanged jokes and pleasantries as I came and went on otherwise dark New York City streets. I don't know. I can't say for sure.

Eric Garner's death was for many in my generation, a moment of (re)awakening. A reminder that over-policing takes many forms, still exists, and sometimes goes beyond harassment (which many in poor, black and brown communities were accustomed to) to murder.

Like many other people, that summer I immersed myself in the news of the time, closely following Eric Garner's story. Would the officers be suspended, arrested? Who would emerge as national spokespeople for this tragedy? And while the Eric Garner story was still unfolding, a few weeks later, news broke of the killing of Michael Brown, Jr. at the hands of police in Ferguson, Missouri. Michael Brown's story helped illuminate the killing of John Crawford III by police in Beavercreek, Ohio. This made for quite the heavy summer. But through it all, I managed to stay engaged in conversations about racism and injustice.

During a trip to visit a friend in Maryland that August, I went to visit the Martin Luther King, Jr. Memorial in Washington, DC for the first time. It opened three years earlier, but the timing of my visit was perfect. I remember crying. It was larger than I thought it would be. And his beautiful carved features seemed to speak to me in some way. At the gift shop, I purchased a copy of his *Letter from Birmingham Jail.*

I spent the next few weeks pondering the activism and organizing tactics that Dr. King described in the book. How much of it was relevant now? How much of it could still be effective now? I thought about my own desire to organize somehow. What would it look like? What groups could I join to amplify the message that Black lives matter? I had so many questions. My heart felt heavy, and my hands felt helpless.

The summer of 2014 wouldn't be the only hot, heavy, helpless summer. Between the summer of 2014 and 2016, there were, unfortunately, numerous other high-profile cases of police violence against Black men and women, including Freddie Carlos Gray, Jr. and Sandra Bland. The list of names just kept growing. And as it did, I grew weary of the viral videos. Being an empath, every instance left a mark on my psyche. I carried the grief of these losses as if I personally knew these men and women. But I didn't. I didn't need to. The awareness that it could have been me or my loved ones was enough.

Then it happened. In the summer of 2016, just two years from when I was consumed, a switch was flipped within me. The numbness set in. I went from feeling everything to making sure I felt nothing. It happened as I watched the viral video of the murder of Philando Castile. I watched in horror, true horror. And my soul couldn't take any more. And I made a conscious decision to avoid all future videos—a decision to avoid clicking on any new hashtags.

Philando Castile was shot by a Minnesota police officer at a routine traffic stop. The officer fired seven shots at Philando as he sat in the driver's seat of his car. Five of the shots hit him. Philando's girlfriend and daughter were in the car with him at the time and could do nothing but watch as the horror (yes, I need to use that word again) unfolded. The police dashcam video, which shows how the situation escalated in less than a minute, and his girlfriend's Facebook live video, which captured Philando bleeding and slumped over, while the visibly shaking and bumbling officer's gun was still trained on him, went viral.

I watched these videos. And decided I was done. Something in me died . . . disconnected. I never wanted to see another video of a Black person, of any person, being killed by police officers. I never wanted to hear another story of some officer thinking they saw a gun, when it was a wallet, a set of keys, or absolutely nothing at all. My emotions, my soul, could not take it. And so I disassociated.

It's here that I'll borrow from the great writer James Baldwin, who once spoke about the constant state of rage that Black people existed in, if they were at all "relatively conscious" ("The Negro in American Culture, *CrossCurrents*, Summer 1961). This is one of those collective responses that I cannot deny.

In the days and weeks following my viewing of those videos of Philando's murder, the overwhelming emotion of being conscious of the treatment of Black people in America was too much for me to handle. I was tired of being in a rage, tired of having a heavy heart and helpless hands. And so, for the next several years, I did everything within me to avoid learning the details about any new instances of violence against Black people at the hands of those in power. This was when I entered my season of numbness.

Disassociation is a psychological term used to describe when someone detaches from an array of physical and emotional experiences. I didn't know that's what was happening at the time. But it was. What started off as a conscious decision to limit my exposure to certain news stories about injustice, grew to include a complete detachment from the news in general—a detachment from any current events happening in the world around me.

The election of President Donald Trump in 2016, and all the violence surrounding his campaign, only further drove my desire to stay away from the news. But in doing so, I became numb. I walked around in a cloud, because it was better than walking around in a state of grief and confusion. Some might call this a coward's way out. I call it self-preservation. And I lived this way—purposely blind to the state of the world around me—every day, for four years.

I emerged from this numbness in 2020, when a rapidly spreading pandemic, COVID-19, began sweeping the globe. The pandemic necessitated my return to partake in conversations about global affairs—once again, for my self-preservation. And it wasn't far into 2020, now being more attentive to news media and social media, before another hashtag began circulating online. The May 25th murder of George Floyd—also in Minnesota, like Philando Castile—shook me to my core. Still sensitive, I could not watch the viral video. But the pictures of a grinning Officer Derek Chauvin kneeling on George's neck as life left his body and the audio of his dying words were enough.

So what is it like to be Black in America? I'm still not sure I've answered that question clearly or specifically. But one thing I can say is that because of the trauma associated with being Black in America (both historic and daily), there is a mental fortitude required to simply exist in this country that not many others will ever understand. A fortitude that we ourselves might not always find tenable. For many years, as discussed here, mine was shaky.

What needs to change, and why is it so important for change to happen sooner than later?

What needs to change? Everything. Yes. Everything. I know this is a general response. But racism is so deeply ingrained in all of America's systems and traditions that a thorough examination, dismantling, and, in many cases, a subsequent reimagining of systems and traditions is necessary.

This country's social and economic systems were built and scaled on the enslavement of Black people in America, which cannot be denied. However, what folks do continue to deny is the more-than-sufficient statistical, anecdotal, and historical evidence demonstrating that although slavery ended, the disenfranchisement of Blacks in America continued with Reconstruction, Jim Crow, and our modern-day criminal justice system. This denial has perpetuated a myth that the reason that Black Americans haven't enjoyed the success that other groups in America have is because Blacks are lazy and refuse to pull themselves up by their bootstraps.

But, in reality, even with our best "bootstrapping" efforts, making the best use of our often limited resources and networks, there have been rules (both spoken and unspoken) and laws (explicitly written and enforced) that are designed to suppress any true marked success. These rules demonstrate an all-out resistance to Black advancement. The fear that Black Americans will somehow outpace white Americans has resulted in violence and the destruction of some of our best efforts toward self-sufficiency as a people. (See the 1917 East St. Louis Massacre, the 1921 Tulsa Race Massacre, the 1923 Rosewood Massacre, and the list goes on.)
And I do mean success "as a people." Not the success of the occasional few who "make it." America needs to have a moment of truth in which it admits that slavery never truly ended, it just changed its form. And for every so-called "leg up" or "handout" that people think Black Americans were given, others were given so much more, so much sooner, along with a centuries-long head start in the

103

proverbial race for achievement. The sooner this nation is able to admit this, the more likely we will be to make some gains against institutional racism.

Why do these changes need to happen now? Well, *now* is always the time to do what's right. To delay these systemic changes means more heartache, more pain, and more helplessness for yet another generation. In *Why We Can't Wait,* Dr. Martin Luther King, Jr. wrote that while fighting for an end to segregation in Birmingham, he was constantly told that the timing of the fight was bad. But he said his opponents failed to realize that "it was ridiculous to speak of timing when the clock of history showed that the Negro had already suffered one hundred years of delay."

When you discover an injustice, you fix it. Period! Even the Bible, in a different context, says that it's foolish for people to look in the mirror, walk away, and immediately forget what they saw (James 1:23–24). Yet this is what we do when it comes to racial inequalities in this country. This is what Dr. King was referring to every time he was told that his timing was bad. It was as if everyone in a position of power, every authority, would look at the injustice and walk away without trying to fix it.

Well, the movement right now, as it was back then, is not about to let those in power and authority walk away from the mirror. We have to make sure issues affecting us remain visible and that the demands remain heard. And we can no longer accept the claims of those who would say "now is not the right time" or that we're asking for too much. Excuses are no longer acceptable, and change cannot be delayed. America has been delaying change by walking away from the mirror for more than one hundred years. Look in the mirror, America. See your flaws. And fix them. Now.

How can we learn more?

An excellent resource that everyone should view is *13th*, a documentary directed by Ava DuVernay. I've written about America's need to understand that slavery has shifted form and that the systems in this country currently support and uphold the continued enslavement of Black people, although it is no longer called "slavery." This documentary traces the history of events and laws from the end of slavery to the modern-day criminal justice system, further demonstrating why this system in particular needs to be dismantled and reimagined sooner rather than later.

I also reference Dr. Martin Luther King, Jr.'s *Letter from Birmingham Jail* as another important resource. We have a burgeoning generation of activists who are protesting injustice right now, because that's all they know to do. But there is, indeed, a method to activist activities. Even if people do not follow Dr. King's tactics, it would be an eyeopener for any novice activist to see the strategy and intent that went into every action taken on the mission to desegregate Birmingham. Activism is sometimes portrayed as emotional and reactionary. But it is quite strategic and intentional.

Biography

Inacent Saunders is a native of Brooklyn, New York, currently living in Phoenix, Arizona. Professionally, she is a nonprofit consultant, dedicating the past twenty-five years of her life to the nonprofit sector. She has a special passion for youth and community development organizations, likely because this is where she cut her teeth in the nonprofit world many years ago as a teenager.

Recognizing the need for knowledgeable, skilled, experienced talent in senior leadership at organizations serving some of society's most vulnerable populations, Saunders pursued and obtained a Master of Science in nonprofit leadership degree from Fordham University in 2017. That same year, she founded Groundwork for

Change LLC, a nonprofit consulting practice, dedicated to ensuring that grassroots organizations have the capacity necessary to launch and scale transformative social-impact initiatives.

A lover of the written and spoken word, Saunders is a published author who enjoys writing in her free time. Her first published work, *From Pain to Praise: The Prose and Poems of a Daughter-in-Process,* is a personal anthology of poems, short stories, and journal entries written throughout her adolescent life, reflecting her long, often painful, road to discovering her identity in Christ. This work has affected young women across the country, many of whom have sought her out for insight in their own lives as young women of faith.

Saunders's faith is important to her. She became a Christian in 2008 and has never looked back. She is an ordained elder and her ministry focus is journeying with people to help them discover their God-given identities. She is excited to do this in whatever way God leads her—not just within the four walls of the church, but also informally in everyday life. She is always doing something new, including working on a new book.

THE PREROGATIVE TO TAKE UP SPACE
Tish Times

While I am grateful to be an American, my heart breaks because it doesn't always feel as though America is grateful for our Black men. I am especially concerned as a mother of three amazing tall Black men and the wife of a kind, yet physically imposing, Black man. I have spent many nights praying for their safety from danger and hoping they never find themselves in a position where they are in police custody.

When I asked the men in my life about their experiences as Black male Americans, my heart broke just a little more.

Derrell's Experiences

Derrell Peoples, my eldest son, describes his experience as a Black man in America as a roller coaster of pride, paranoia, and pain. He says that as a six-foot-two, dark-skinned Black male with bold features, it often seems like people are threatened by his presence. Things that should never happen to other humans have become predictable behavior to him. Wary conduct, such as people avoiding eye contact or a woman clutching her purse, has become the daily expectation for my thirty-year-old son.

Derrell says that his experiences with racism have hardened him to the point of numbness. Being profiled and feared should not be the norm but they are. Unfortunately, the numbness has become the armor necessary just to live.

It's important, Derrell says, to acknowledge that people aren't born full of hate and racism. It's possible that if the new generation can act by leading with love, the views passed down by older generations will slowly dissolve. People need to diligently do independent research to understand our history and try to see from the eyes of the "oppressed."

A few good documentaries that Derrell recommends are *LA 92,* directed by Daniel Lindsay and T. J. Martin about the riots in Los Angeles following the Rodney King verdict; *When They See Us,* a TV miniseries created by Ava DuVernay: and *13th,* directed by Ava DuVernay, an in-depth look into how the Thirteenth Amendment contributes to the mass incarceration of Black people. Derrell also suggests *Time: The Kalief Browder Story* directed by Jenner Furst, produced by Jay-Z. However, he warns that it might cause you to lose faith in any hope of life ever being fair and equal for everyone.

Derrell believes that becoming aware of some of the atrocities people still face in 2020 should be so maddening that you have no other option except to spring forward into some type of action.

Lavell's Story

My twenty-eight-year-old son, Lavell Jones, declares that it's important to say that Black people are proud to be Black. However, being Black in America means having to work twice as hard while receiving half the recognition and constantly having to prove you're not a criminal. Being Black in America is tiring, to say the least, Lavell says.

Lavell states that the system doesn't feel just and equal for all. He thinks that change is necessary because for generations Black people have dealt with oppression. Though in different forms throughout the years, it is still happening.

Hidden Colors: The Untold History of People of Aboriginal, Moor, and African Descent, directed by Tariq Nasheed, is a great documentary that Lavell recommends to educate people about Black history and racial injustice. Being informed is important, but then action is required.

Charles's Story

My twenty-one-year-old son, Charles Times, believes that being a Black man in America feels like there is a target on your back at all times. Charles tells of times when he was followed in stores when shopping. He spoke of how his heart pumps erratically when a police officer is behind him while driving. He also mentions a constant state of alert for fear of what someone will see when they look at him. Charles describes the discomfort with knowing that someone can create whatever narrative they come up with about him, true or not, and that story could result in a police officer taking his life.

Roy's Story

My husband, Roy Times, believes being Black in America is a combination of being second-guessed, marginalized, and feared. People assume you are dangerous; they assume you are a threat. But when they take the time to know you, they are surprised you are educated, intelligent, and capable, he explains.

My husband understands that we can't change people's hearts, but we can change the systems that promote the oppression of minority groups. Systemic racism should not be the standard for how business is done. Roy believes that, unfortunately, racism is woven into the fabric of how certain institutions operate. He points out that redlining and gerrymandering still happen. Social media and video have made it more difficult to deny what has been taking place for years. Each person must take personal responsibility to say, "I am going to fight against the oppression of minority groups."

Tish's Summary

Something that all the men in my family expressed is the need to soften their voices or their smiles intentionally, just to appear more friendly and minimize the perception of threat.

As a mother who has taught her children how to govern themselves in social settings, it is disheartening to know that their behavior has frequently been influenced by racism. It's almost as if Black people are forced to be ultra-polite just to be accepted, to avoid arrest, or, in some cases, to save their own lives. I'm concerned (for all our children) that they will begin to believe that they don't have the prerogative to take up space as themselves.

Biography

Tish Times is the founder of Tish Times Networking & Sales Training. She is a certified networker, community builder, and franchise owner for Network in Action in Phoenix, Arizona. For nearly ten years, Times has been teaching small business owners, solo entrepreneurs, and sales professionals to increase income with unparalleled sales and networking strategies. Times empowers sales professionals to create revenue-generating business connections, follow-up effectively, stay top-of-mind, shorten the sales cycle, and close sales with ease.

Times's books include *Networking Is Not a One-Night Stand: A Guide for Building Lasting Business Relationships, The Unstoppable Confidence Networking Playbook: A Planning Tool to Maximize Your Networking Efforts and Boost Your Bottom Line, OMG! 10 Super Simple Steps for Career Success,* and *The Networking & Sales Planner.*

Times is the founder of the Unstoppable Confidence Networking & Sales Academy, a business school that teaches a systematic, sincere, and effective approach to networking and sales to produce lucrative bottom-line results.

YIELD TO THE WHITENESS AROUND YOU
LaWanna R. Wilson

To be Black in America is to be chronically apologetic about your existence. Being from a Christian home, I have been taught to be polite and well-mannered. As I grew up, I noticed what I would call hyper-polite behavior that Black people showed around whites. For example, if you are in a store and the aisle is narrow, the Black person yields to the white person and waits for them to pass first. Or if you are at work in a meeting and you and a white coworker begin to speak simultaneously, the Black person yields the floor to the white person to continue his or her comment first. These are just small examples.

To be Black in America is to constantly find yourself in situations where you have to "choose your battles." You have to decide if it's worth the hassle and the ostracizing that will follow if you assert yourself, your right to "be" in any way, and be labeled aggressive, insubordinate, or hostile or if you should, once again, be apologetic and polite and yield to the whiteness around you.

What needs to change, and why is it so important for change to happen sooner than later?

Whiteness as the default preference must be changed. We must dismantle the structures and systems that support this preference and work toward a genuine equality, acceptance, and celebration of uniqueness and diversity where all ethnic groups are deemed valuable and necessary.

How can we learn more?

There is a number of recommended books I could list, including *White Fragility: Why It's So Hard for White People to Talk about Racism* by Robin DiAngelo; *A Black Women's History of the United States* by Daina Ramey Berry and Kali Nicole Gross; and *How to Be an Antiracist* by Ibram X Kendi. I also recommend the 2016 documentary *I Am Not Your Negro* directed by Raoul Peck, based on an unfinished manuscript by James Baldwin.

In addition, social media accounts that have been helpful are The AND Campaign, LiveFreeUSA, Grassroots Law Project, and Equal Justice Initiative (EJI). The replay for the virtual JusticeCon conference was extremely insightful and can be viewed on YouTube. These resources, for me and many others, have given insight, factual information, and practical steps about the root issues, along with a variety of practical steps to protest, support, and communicate with clarity our demands.

Biography

LaWanna R. Wilson is a speaker and author. She possesses a Bachelor of Arts in speech and dramatic arts degree from Fisk University in Nashville, Tennessee. Upon graduation, she continued her love of music and speaking by hosting a morning drive-time radio show at WFLT in her hometown of Flint, Michigan. She continued to refine her writing skill by producing local stage plays and songs.

Wilson's love for writing began in third grade with journaling. It was then that she began to dream of writing books. Her first book, *V.I.R.G.I.N.*, was birthed from a desire to start a conversation that she felt was rarely happening between her generation, Millennials, and the Gen Z generation regarding their worth and embracing their individual uniqueness. Her focus is to give them insight into the real world by using her personal experiences as an example to help them identify and develop their strengths and utilize those strengths to benefit their communities and their world. She interacts with them via workshops, small group discussions, and her weekly online live broadcast.

Wilson has a heart for international outreach. She has served as a full-time missionary and her travels have taken her as far as Namibia. She has found in her travels that no matter where she goes, young people need someone to look them in the eye and remind them that they are seen, they have worth, and they can make a difference in the world.

ALL AMERICA SEES IS THE COLOR OF MY SKIN
Artesian Kirksey

What is it like to be Black in America?

It is frustrating. I am probably not the first person to say this, but being Black in America is frustrating. Being Black in America is also exhausting. From a Black male's perspective, no matter what your socioeconomic status is, you are immediately assumed to be a threat because of the color of your skin.

I am a living example of this, as I grew up in an inner city that was predominately populated by Blacks. I noticed the police then would patrol the neighborhoods like zookeepers versus the suburban community I live in now where they actually serve and protect. It does not matter that I am a US Marine, a college professor, an administrator, professional speaker, and an author. All America sees is the color of my skin and what it supposedly represents.

I remember a few years ago, as I was driving my kids to school, I was pulled over before I even left my subdivision. The officer said he pulled me over because I was driving two miles over the speed limit. He let me off with a warning but not before asking, "What do you do for a living?" The reason he asked was because I was driving a BMW 7 Series.

I asked, "What does my occupation have to do with anything?"

He replied, "There have been people in my subdivision selling drugs," implying that I had to be one of "those people" because I was driving this type of vehicle.

Unfortunately, I have experienced many encounters like this. No matter how much I have accomplished or whichever affluent neighborhood my wife and I choose to raise our family, whenever I get pulled over by a police officer, I automatically assume the worst-case scenario will occur. The police officer looks for any reason to take me in or use excessive force, whereas my white counterpart's only fear might be the financial obligation he is burdened with as a result of this encounter.

What needs to change, and why is it so important for change to happen sooner than later?

We need to start our change with the US Constitution. It needs to be completely rewritten—this time, making sure Black people are included. Another change we can implement immediately is police reform and more effective police training—more specifically, diversity and sensitivity training. I also think that police should be able to work in similar communities, like where they grew up, but not the same communities. In my opinion, that is a conflict of interest.

For example, if I grew up in Milwaukee, Wisconsin, I should only be able to police in communities with a similar demographic, but not in Milwaukee. I believe this would alleviate many senseless killings of Black people. This could build trust between police and the Black community.

It is important that this happens soon, because it is long overdue, and people are getting restless. We are at a boiling point in society. If things do not change soon, I fear the worst might be yet to come.

How can we learn more?

The 2016 documentary, *MILWAUKEE 53206*, directed by Keith McQuirter, chronicles three intimate stories of Milwaukee residents who received excessive and racially biased jail sentences. It examines the high toll and stress that it has on the individuals, their families, and the communities they come from. It discusses how the United States has the most prisoners of any nation in the world in both absolute numbers and per capita. These numbers are further compounded within Milwaukee's mostly African American 53206 ZIP Code, where 62 percent of adult Black men are currently in prison or have served time.

I recommend this film for people who are looking to understand systemic racism and want to gain a perspective on what it is like to be targeted strictly based on skin color. Once people watch this film, I think they will have a better awareness and understanding of what Black people go through on a day-to-day basis. The hope is that this will prompt them to take action when they see injustices occurring. This would consciously allow them to be a part of the solution instead of unconsciously being part of the problem.

All in all, I believe Dr. Martin Luther King, Jr.'s "I Have a Dream" speech is closer to a reality today than it has ever been, but we still have work to do. I am keeping hope alive for all future generations.

Biography

Artesian Kirksey is a transformational speaker and mental skills coach who helps people marry their potential to the right mentality. A trained higher education professional, transformational speaker, and mental skills coach, Kirksey has a unique fifteen-year background in educational leadership, instruction, organizational management, and strategic planning. Over the span of his career, he has had the extreme pleasure of working with students from all walks of life and guiding them throughout the various phases of their college experiences. He has been fortunate enough to have had the opportunity to serve as a college professor, dean of faculty, and dean of academic affairs.

Kirksey, a US Marine and active member of the community, is the founder and chief executive officer (CEO) of Artwork, LLC—the leading content provider in mindset development training and curriculum. He attributes much of his success and overall character development to his experiences in the Marine Corps. The leadership traits that were instilled in him during his time in the military provided a solid foundation for his current mission: to transform lives, one mindset at a time. Kirksey is the author of *The Art of Transformation: Eight Practical Tips to Help You Marry Your Potential to the Right Mentality*.

THE ULTIMATE DICHOTOMY
Jaylynn Tamela Smith

Being Black in America is a culmination of the best and the worst of experiences at the same time. Our culture is expressive, creative, and glowing. We have bodied nearly every arena we find ourselves in. From the arts to neighborhoods and homes, from the richest of sectors to the poorest, Black people create the whole vibe. I love having Black skin and hair that can do almost anything. I love the energy that we bring to the table on every level.

But being Black in America also acknowledges the worst parts of this country. It is constantly proving our worth and protecting our energy. It means that we are hated and feared for being beautiful. It's constantly seeing death and poverty forced into our communities only to be gaslighted by those who created the system to exploit our condition.

Being Black in America is the ultimate dichotomy. It's carrying the weight of both pride and grief at the same time and balancing them all while trying to make it home alive to see those you love one more day.

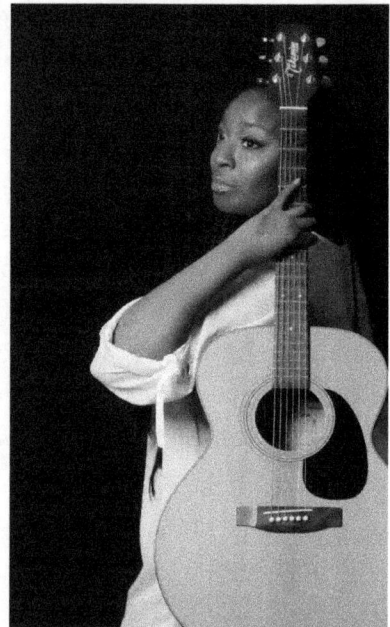

What needs to change, and why is it so important for change to happen sooner than later?

We need to change this system. We need to break it down to the core of its foundation. Whenever we seek to change the core elements that this country was built on, there are people who will try to pacify us with symbolism. I recall when my child was small and I would take something away from her, she would cry. I would sometimes try to give her something else to distract her from crying. The way that these entities respond to our pain lets me know how little I'm thought of. It's like they are trying to trick a crying toddler into being interested in something else while they let what we want slip from our fingers.

The system needs to change now because the more we realize that we aren't being heard—that the efforts are merely an attempt to pacify—the more offended we will become. We are looking at historic levels of outrage, and these current quick fixes are just bringing our emotions to a boiling point. That's not what we want.

How can we learn more?

I think that D. L. Hughley is an excellent resource for foundational understanding. His views aren't as political as they are social. Hughley has practical solutions and actionable items that the common individual can follow with ease. Being able to understand and deliver are crucial in these present times.

Biography

Jaylynn Tamela Smith is the founder and director of MacC Yes Total Health Corporation, a 501(c)3 corporation that works to educate and empower the people of the Greater Phoenix Area in the area of mental health through the pathway of advocacy and education. She is also the pastor of The Gathering Small Group Worship, an Acts 2, trauma-informed church focused on edification and relationship building. She is the author of *Be Anxious for Nothing*, along with other books in the series related to Christian mental health.

WE CANNOT TURN A BLIND EYE
Simone E. Morris

In 2020, the color of my Black (brown) skin matters. It matters for the entire race. It doesn't matter the heights you reach; it simply matters and has a causal effect based on said existence. I reflect on how proud I was of former President Barack Obama for being President of the United States. His experiences played out in front of us—some positive and some extremely negative. The questioning of his heritage and leadership had the underlying tone that there was still resistance to the color of his skin in such a pivotal role. Enemies got in his way and made the journey painful. We continued to root for his success. And in 2020, as we make comparisons of leadership then and now, it is clear that he was truly an inclusive leader and that there was a penalty to pay. As a Jamaican who immigrated to the United States in 1979, my identity is strong. When I'm classified as an African American, there is a sense that I don't belong.

To be Black in America means that you have to show proof of who you are to thrive. This proof could be in the form of attire, education, work, and more. It's disheartening. Any indication of wrongful death creates a wave of fear that it's creeping closer and closer, and it's downright scary for Black families. We worry deeply about our loved ones (especially the males) as we see more and more footage of police brutality that shows us we are not safe.

What needs to change, and why is it so important for change to happen sooner than later?

1. There needs to be more inclusive leadership in the White House. Leadership needs to model inclusion, and, unfortunately, that isn't happening right now. It feels like politics need an entire overhaul. This is a huge opportunity that needs more than fixing voting. We cannot turn a blind eye to despicable behavior. Yet, that's what's happening. This needs to stop in 2020.

2. Inclusive leadership must be a lesson for everyone. The onus is not just on organizations to teach others to be inclusive. The onus is on us all to care about the entire human race. We need to use our influence to teach others and to shine a light on injustices that need our help to be corrected.

3. Schools need to change their curriculum. It needs to be broadened. School leaders need to be held accountable for inclusion. They must be tasked with creating inclusive cultures (leadership, parents, activities, etcetera).

4. Organizations need to be held accountable for the part they play in creating an inclusive country. Yes, there's investment in diversifying the workplace. Yes, there are attempts to create inclusive cultures. There must still be more consistent work and support to continue to sustain inclusion.

How can we learn more?

The killings of Ahmaud Arbery and George Floyd moved me in a way that I could no longer sit idly by and not use my influence to bring awareness and bring a change forward. That was the catalyst for me. The human in me could not tolerate this unnecessary loss. I felt it with Trayvon Martin's death, but it was a different level than George Floyd's death. I think it's the compilation of racial injustice and that it's still happening in 2020 that has been so pivotal for me. It is beyond unacceptable, and change must happen. I have to be a part of creating change for the future generation.

Biography

Simone E. Morris is chief executive officer (CEO) of Simone Morris Enterprises LLC, a certified minority and women-owned business enterprise. She is an award-winning diversity and inclusion leader and a consultant and speaker committed to training women and emerging leaders to take true leadership positions in all aspects of their lives. She is proud of her work to educate companies to walk in integrity when it comes to inclusive leadership.

Morris has a background that includes over two decades in corporate America, spanning information technology, commercial strategy, and human resources. She holds a Master's in Business Administration (MBA) degree from the University of Connecticut. Her technology background has served her well, embedding strong project management acumen that allows her to educate and create transformational results for her clients. She teaches diversity and inclusion, conscious inclusion, and project management.

Morris shares her message across various platforms (for example, *Entrepreneur, Forbes,* The Good Men Project, Medium, Thrive Global, Glassdoor, Leadercast, SmartRecruiters, Social Hire, Diversity Best Practices, *Profiles in Diversity Journal,* and BambooHR). She is the author of *52 Tips for Owning Your Career: Practical Advice for Career Success, The Power of Owning Your Career: Winning Strategies, Tools and Tips for Creating Your Desired Career,* and *Achievement Unlocked: Strategies to Set Goals and Manifest Them.*

She resides in Connecticut with her family.

WHITE AMERICA HAS A 400-YEAR HEAD START

Dr. Helen Holton

I was born Black in America. It's the lens through which I live, breathe, and have my being. I am a child of God. The context of my existence is shaped by four hundred years of bondage, oppression, and exclusion. Systemic racism, conscious and unconscious bias, white privilege, and greed have perpetuated and sustained an inequitable societal construct targeted and placed on Black people in America.

On April 12, 2015, a twenty-five-year-old Black man in Baltimore was arrested and taken into police custody. Not an uncommon occurrence in too many neighborhoods across America. On April 19, 2015, that young Black man, Freddie Carlos Gray, Jr., took his last breath while in custody of the police. By this time, Freddie Gray was in the hospital, in a coma, as a result of injuries sustained while in police custody.

What does it mean to be Black in America? It means that the value placed on your life as a Black person in America carries a false narrative of "less than, not good enough, and dispensable." Unfortunately, this demise of too many Black people doesn't agitate us enough to be like civil rights activist Fannie Lou Hamer who declared, "I'm sick and tired of being sick and tired."

The day Freddie Gray died changed my life for the better. As a senior member of the Baltimore City Council, it was an awkward and painful awakening. It challenged me as a leader in many ways. The duty, responsibility, and accountability to the tribe of Black people in America and throughout the diaspora is real and nothing to take lightly.

The events that took place following Freddie Gray's funeral on Monday, April 27, are still fresh in my memory like it was yesterday; hard to believe it's been five years. It was an overcast afternoon. After spending hours inside the church for a politically charged and emotional farewell, it was refreshing to stand and breathe fresh air outdoors. The climate outside was anything but calm. There was a storm brewing, an uneasiness, and I could feel it in the atmosphere.

People often lament the death of young people. It defies the natural order of life, even more so for Black people. There was a buzz in the air with reports about rioting to begin soon at a neighboring school. Frederick Douglass High School, a few blocks from the church, was situated across a major thoroughfare from the historic Mondawmin Mall, one of the oldest shopping centers in the country still open today. It is also a major mass transit transfer station for public transportation riders. The majority of public school students in Baltimore City ride public transportation to reach their schools, many of whom change bus lines at Mondawmin Mall.

City Council meetings are held on Mondays at five P.M., with the exception of two times a year when there's a mandated meeting held on a Thursday, once in June and once in December. Hearing rumors about an uprising as a way to bring attention to the wrongful death of Freddie Gray while in police custody never sounded like something that would ensue in the next few hours. It was a city council meeting day and the disruption to a normal Monday routine meant I needed to play catchup before the start of the council meeting.

Back in the office, going through phone messages, emails, and snail mail, to prepare for the evening council meeting, my assistant came in and turned on my television to alert me to chaos in the city. Before my eyes, I watched the emergence of an uprising in my beloved city. The footage of confrontation between young Black people and the police was surreal. The pharmacy, one in the largest chain of pharmacies in America, went up in flames. The protest, increased destruction, and violence progressed through a swath of Baltimore and lasted deep into the night.

Freddie Gray's death unleashed a wave of pent-up frustration and disgust over the realities of what it means to be Black in America. The disrespect, discrimination, and abuse of Black people must stop. The systems constructed to deny us and keep us down must come to an end.

Sandtown-Winchester, the neighborhood where Freddie Gray lived, has been a longstanding beneficiary of government and philanthropic giving. The millions of dollars invested in brick-and-mortar aesthetics haven't made a significant difference in the lives of marginalized Black people in the community. Putting a bandage on a wound that is hemorrhaging is not a viable solution.

As I sat in my office that Monday afternoon in a daze over what was unfolding, my mind kept telling me, *This doesn't make sense. How is this happening? What did we miss?* The travesty of this story is its reflection of the benign neglect that's taking place across America in predominantly Black neighborhoods. It affects education through the condition of our schools. It affects economics through the challenges of employment and earning a living wage, to safe and affordable housing, to food and safe drinking water. The interconnectedness of systems complicates the challenge even more.

131

The tragic and senseless deaths of Black people in our communities reveals the ugly, naked truth of systemic racism, unconscious bias, and white privilege displayed in some of the most depraved acts of unnecessary and unwarranted violence and hatred. We see it all around us every day. In many ways, we have become blind to the injustice it represents.

The unjustified murders of Black people by police is why we must continue to press for justice, equity, inclusion, equality, and opportunity. We must not grow weary in well-doing. We must speak their names and remember them. We must know our history and teach it to our children, so they will never take for granted our fight for freedom.

The COVID-19 pandemic is the most significant global paradigm shift of the century. In an indiscriminate way, it has shown us that race, ethnicity, class, sexual orientation, and whatever other classifications of separation we can muster don't matter to the coronavirus. It's an equal opportunity virus for which no one gets a pass. We are all susceptible to it. It's an equalizer of sorts. It's a wakeup call. We are all in this mess together, and our best hope for getting out is to work together.

There is good news. When I was growing up, we were told by the elders that to make it in this life we would have to work harder, smarter, and faster to get ahead. Let's face it, to be Black in America means that I belong to a group of resilient people who continue to press for better. White America has a four-hundred-year head start. However, where there is hope, there is opportunity for better.

"We are the ones we have been waiting for."

—June Jordan, "Poem for South African Women"

What needs to change, and why is it so important for change to happen sooner than later?

What needs to change first is our attitude. We must believe we deserve better before we can begin to actualize such a reality. It requires focused intention, commitment, and discipline. It demands a collective and collaborative effort. The Montgomery Bus Boycott lasted 381 days in 1955–1956, thirteen consecutive months. It began a major national push toward fairness and equal treatment. Many of the freedoms we take for granted were paid with the price of life.

Educating our children about the rich history and heritage of Black people is a wonderful place to begin. That job rests on the shoulders of every Black adult. When we send our children to school to be educated, it's our responsibility to hold them accountable for the quality of the education. This is where voting and participating in the US Census become important pieces of the equation of justice, equity, equality, and inclusion. We must advocate and agitate for what's right and fair.

Time waits for no one. Each time we find ourselves as a people violated by the structures of society is a wake-up call for action. When we consider the impact of George Floyd, Breonna Taylor, Sandra Bland, Ahmaud Arbery, Oscar Grant, Renisha McBride, and Freddie Gray, they each in some way with their lives and tragic deaths are opportunities to do something. Speak their names!

Write a letter to your local, state, and federal representatives. Ask them what they are doing to improve your community. How are they representing the injustices we face? Do you know where the people you elect to represent you stand on Black Lives Matter?

Now is the time to upshift your engagement with the people and things you encounter every day that affect your life and livelihood. What's your next move forward toward justice for Black people?

How can we learn more?

Reading is fundamental. Today, there's so much information available and whether you like holding a book in your hand or reading from your smart device or listening to books, there's no excuse not to engage with a good book for information and knowledge.

One of the most powerful books I have ever read as a Black person was *Chains and Images of Psychological Slavery* by Na'im Akbar, PhD, clinical psychologist. It's a wonderful primer and a relatively quick read. Its title says it all.

Moving from awareness to action begins with being awake to the conditions that keep us down and get in the way of our greatness. Be intentional about everything you do. Information is power, however, it doesn't become powerful until we put it to use. Untapped knowledge lives within each one of us. What are you willing to do consistently to increase your awareness?

We live in a time where there's no shortage of information. I encourage you to consider the source of your information and use it responsibly for good and not evil. There's far too much evil going around these days.

Biography

Helen Holton is a recovering elected official after twenty-one years of service on the Baltimore City Council. An original thought leader and subject matter expert on the power of inclusion, resilience, and respect, Holton knows that investment in talent is key. As a result, this leader in business, public policy, and nonprofit sectors founded Dr. Helen Holton and Associates, a collaborative organization of forward-thinking minds committed to deepening engagements for better outcomes. Her mindset naturally moves from what's wrong to what's strong!

Holton is an exceptional coach, consultant, and communicator who works to shift the trajectory of success to new heights. Her expertise lives in the intercultural perspective of local issues with global impact; focused at the intersection of race, gender, political power, and privilege. She brings authentic truths, beliefs, and perspectives to situations without personal attachment. She speaks to what's not being said from a sincere space of curiosity and inquisitiveness. The intention is to evoke a deeper level of real, vulnerable, and honest engagement in the work she does with leaders, teams, and organizations. The result is a stronger return on investment (ROI) and an optimal internal rate of return (IRR) produced from the investment in human capital to build and strengthen more inclusive, resilient, and respectful environments.

To every engagement, Holton brings complementary business skills as a certified public accountant (CPA), a master in business administration degree, and a professional in human resources by the Society for Human Resource Management—Certified Professional (PHR/SHRM-CP), holding several coaching certifications and credentialed through the International Coach Federation (ICF) as a professional certified coach and mentor coach. She is a Gallup-Certified Strengths Coach and Trainer, qualified administrator of the Intercultural Development Inventory (IDI), Certified Personal and Executive Coach (CPEC), and Certified Professional Co-Active Coach (CPCC).

Holton's life work and passion in business (for-profit and nonprofit), politics, public policy, and ministry result in a unique blend of head and heart, resulting in an unparalleled experience for those she works with. The convergence of these disciplines is reflected in how she shows up for engagements with technical expertise and compassion in a holistic body, mind, and spirit encounter. She is a natural coach, teacher, mentor, and advisor who took these talents to another level as a practitioner of leadership coaching and professional development. She holds several certifications in personal, professional, and executive leadership coaching and is credentialed through the ICF.

BEFORE ALL LIVES MATTER, BLACK LIVES MUST MATTER
Chandra Gore

To be Black in America is a double-edged sword. I am a Black woman in a country that does not even want to acknowledge the existence of my being or the struggles that I go through on a daily basis as a human being. The fact I have to fight so hard to have my voice heard, to be understood, to not be looked at as a threat, or to not be welcome is one of the hardest parts of being Black in America.

We have to struggle to find doctors who believe us when we say we are in pain or that we even suffer from mental health issues because, at times, those issues are usually down-played and not acknowledged at all.

Even when we are passionate or if we express ourselves, we are known as the angry Black person or argumentative or aggressive, and it is so disappointing that we have to walk that fine line to be able to simply exist because if we are quiet, it's a problem; if we protest or express ourselves, it's an issue. So being in a space where you are constantly policing yourself becomes tiring. Even for our children, at times, being Black becomes a burden as they have to deal with the various issues that come along with being this color that no one chooses

and as they walk on eggshells just to be sure that no violence will be exhibited towards them.

The question of what it's like to be Black in America is a mirror of emotion and a lot of it is pain and misunderstanding on why the simple hue of my skin is such an issue. When you can be murdered while lying in bed asleep like Breonna Taylor, it makes no sense that a death can be just ignored, and the people who murdered you are able to walk free knowing they that no one will avenge your death or get justice for your family. This girl was twenty-three years old, an essential worker, and a hardworking person, yet they burst in and shot her while she was sleeping.

Had she been white, you know there would be so much outrage. "Oh my gosh! You went in and killed her?!" There wouldn't be the sentiment of "Oh, you know. It was a drug house." There wouldn't be excuse after excuse after excuse with a prosecutor not understanding that this is murder no matter the skin tone.

Being Black in America is knowing that your husband, your wife, your child, your son, your daughter, your aunt, your uncle, your grandmother, or your grandfather can walk outside and just check the mail; or just play in a park; or just go for a walk to bird watch or walk the dog; or just buy a snack at a convenience store … and they can be murdered. And their death would mean nothing. Being Black in America is one of the hardest jobs. We have to police our feelings, and we have to take the time to explain to our babies what they can't do. But it comes innate to you, as a Black person, as innate as you wiping your head, putting your hands in your pocket, or even talking or being expressive or being happy or running around playing, and all the while they have to be mindful of their surroundings.
Seriously, being Black in America is tiresome. It's a burden no one should have to live in such conditions to where you are constantly on edge. It's traumatic, and this

has to stop. The narrative must change. Everybody should be treated equally. When someone says "all lives matter," it is as if they do not realize there are citizens of this country who have been shown that their lives do *not* matter. Justice has to be served for those who've been murdered. Justice has to be served for families to heal from seeing their loved ones murdered over and over again on national news to play out as if it's normal is just wrong. Before all lives matter, Black lives have to matter.

What needs to change, and why is it so important for change to happen sooner than later?

Change has to happen. The dismissing of Black women has to stop—from doctors to employers, it must stop. There has to be policy change, legislative overhaul of laws in place, and the hearts and minds of those who are in power must also change because without this, we will continue to have the issues that we have. Without these changes we will continue to have two different justice systems, and what is currently going on will continue and become progressively worse.

We're in the middle of dealing with so much as a country for there to be this amount of disgust for peaceful protests that are happening so that people are made aware of the lives that are taken and the lack acknowledging that people of color are valuable—that their lives matter. The fact that there are judges and prosecutors who dole out to Blacks unreasonable inhumane sentences for crimes that Caucasian counterparts would not even be presented with is wrong. The change has to start on local and state levels, then the federal level. For everyone to matter, these things have to change so people can see us as a country where there is a level field.

There should not be an instance of families being torn apart because there's a law in place that would destroy them. Another huge change would be to label white supremacy groups as terrorist groups and monitor them like they watch other groups that are not creating or promoting hate.

These are the changes that have to come. There has to be a reason—a change—that confirms this kind of behavior is not acceptable. There has to be a precedent set that no matter what, you can be safe inside your home, be safe inside your neighborhood, be safe to own property, to walk this Earth, and not have to worry about someone thinking that they have to police you and check to see if you really belong there. The change has to be made on a personal level and on a mindset level. That is the biggest change that needs to happen.

How can we learn more?

People can learn more by looking at the world from the views of others who are different from them. Instead of minimizing or dismissing the struggle of those who are oppressed, Face the reality that it does exist and that it has to change.

A book that should serve as a resource for others is *The Origin of Others* by Toni Morrison. In this book, Morrison provides questions and helps to find answers based on her memories, books she has read, and what has transpired within the political milestones within the country. She discusses some of her most memorable works as well.

History lessons within this country have romanticized slavery and oppression. This book has helped me gain another perspective and understand that racial injustice is something that should be spoken about and that a change must come.

Biography

Integrity and hard work have always been the hallmarks Chandra has used to build successful and profitable businesses. Through her boutique consulting and public relations firm, Chandra Gore Consulting, she has worked with entrepreneurs to help them create foundations for success through her boutique consulting and public relations firm. Quietly making strides with placements for small businesses, entertainment, authors, therapists and motivational speaking clients on local and national news outlets, she has been leaving her mark as a publicist in the industry. She is also an author, speaker, podcast host, and festival founder and producer.

She also heads a production company, SCM Productions, which produces live comedic events and an upcoming comedy series, "They Said What?!", that will be launched strictly on Amazon. Hosting her successful inaugural comedy festival, Greater Northern Virginia Comedy and Film Festival in 2019, she has anchored herself as a woman to watch in comedy. With a strong feeling of pride in her community, she founded The Urban Flight Foundation to help spread pertinent information, host voter registration drives, and more within the Stafford County, Virginia. She is an author of several books and a moderator and speaker on topics such as business strategies, media relations, and entrepreneurship. Launching Conversations with Chan is her personal brand that includes a podcast, YouTube channel, and a publication on Medium.com.

LEVEL THE PLAYING FIELD
Dr. Shawn Dandridge, Sr.

Being Black in America is not easy. That sentence could serve as the summation of this entire writing. Since the killing of George Floyd on May 25, 2020, the country has seen thousands of marches and protests. Many cities experienced looting and police precincts have even come under attack with some being burned. The country is experiencing a call to end police brutality and racism unlike anything seen since the 1960s with the civil right marches. Exacerbating problems, the COVID-19 pandemic has hit the Black community extremely hard in terms of total deaths and those infected.

In 2020, what is the real pandemic? Is it COVID-19 or racism? I can easily make the argument it is both. The climate is right for change in America. The masses seem to be awakening to the unfair and indifferent treatment of Blacks. When an unarmed Black person is killed, it does not always make the front page of the newspaper anymore as the incidents have been all too common.

The most recent deaths of Black people have set off a Black Lives Matter movement. A few I will mention here include Breonna Taylor, killed while asleep; George Floyd, knee to the neck; Ahmaud Arbery, on an afternoon jog; and Rayshard Brooks, sleeping while intoxicated. Watching so many of the videos almost seems

143

like a movie being played at the cinema. We can become desensitized to inhumane treatment after viewing the innumerable hours of people dying at the hands of police. Then we have to realize, "Wait a minute. This is not a movie; this is right here on American streets." I have had emotions that ranged from rage to hurt and even momentarily at times thinking about inflicting harm back on them.

Richmond, Virginia, has been a city filled with racial unrest, even serving as the home of the capital of the Confederacy in the 1860s. In recent weeks, Confederate monuments have been removed at the urging of Mayor Levar Stoney. This effort by the mayor to take down statues that many consider offensive and racist has led to an outcry by the white community. Lawsuits are pending and temperatures are raging to put the statues back. There are social media comments by many locals commenting on recent events, such as "A civil war is on the way, could easily be found."

Racial inequality in America has always been unsettling. I have experienced it in my own life. The first time I was called a racial slur was in middle school. As a teenager, I got into trouble with the law. During the court hearing, things were said to me by the judge and the prosecutor that were unnecessary and meant to intimidate and scare me. I faced many challenges because of a criminal background. While I do not excuse my immature and criminal behavior as a teen, it cannot be understated the issue of disparity that Blacks face in the criminal justice system.

If convicted felons cannot vote—and many Blacks, by an early age, are felons—then there is a large portion of the population who has to sit idly by when elections occur. A democracy is not a true democracy when millions lack the ability to participate in the election process of American leaders.

What needs to change, and why is it so important for change to happen sooner than later?

A few of the changes I will work tirelessly toward are ending white supremacy, eradicating greed and corruption in governments, curbing police brutality, changing criminal injustice, stopping mass incarceration, fixing inequality in the education system, and gaining equal access for the basic necessities largely absent in Black communities. While all of these are lofty goals, many of them are intertwined with one another and fixing any of them will greatly help people of color.

The systemic racism in America is real and present. As a Black person, I am not asking for freebies, but I do want a level playing field. I believe every Black person in America who descended from slaves should be given reparations. If plantation owners were given money for losing their plantations, then the descendants of slaves should be paid for the back-breaking work of their ancestors.

Education will be key for people of color to achieve better jobs and opportunities. The school-to-prison pipeline has to be corrected. Proper funding of schools must happen. Overcrowding of schools needs to be addressed. Providing equal access to computers and Wi-Fi for all students in all school systems should be a priority. Teachers need to be properly trained and certified. Pay increases for teachers is a must, as many leave the field due to inadequate pay. Students no longer need to be bullied or handcuffed by onsite resource officers for petty offenses and minor common mishaps.

School, churches, and individual homes need to teach the real history of America. For far too long, history books have been whitewashed. Financial literacy needs to become mandatory curriculum and also teaching Spanish as a second language to all students in public schools. Exercise and physical activity have to be part of school activities. Kids are out of shape and unhealthy unlike any time in history. More diversity in local, state, and federal governments would better reflect our communities.

How can we learn more?

I implore you to read *The New Jim Crow: Mass Incarceration in the Age of Colorblindness* by Michelle Alexander. This book gives major insights into the unfair criminal system in America. We used to say the judicial system was broken, but, in hindsight, the system is doing exactly what it was designed to do, and that is to tear apart Black families. Furthermore, it was to keep many from participating in voting, although there are other harmful lasting effects of this process.

One other reading I highly recommend, because it is written by a Caucasian woman with a perspective that is largely uncommon among her race, is *White Fragility: Why It's So Hard for White People to Talk about Racism* by Robin DiAngelo.

Biography

Shawn Dandridge, Sr. resides in Hanover County, Virginia. As a lifelong resident, he attended public schools, kindergarten through twelfth grade. Continuing his education, he attended J. Sargeant Reynolds Community College and Virginia Commonwealth University before completing a degree in business administration at Averett University. In 2012, he earned a Master of Divinity degree from Liberty University. He obtained a Master of Science degree from Virginia Commonwealth University in 2014 along with four units of continuing professional education. In 2020, he graduated from Asbury Theological Seminary in Wilmore, Kentucky, with a Doctor of Ministry.

Dandridge was licensed to preach in 1995 by First Shiloh Baptist Church in Mechanicsville, Virginia, with Rev. R. Neal Siler, pastor. He has been involved in prison ministry outreach since 1996 and continues to the present. From 1999 to 2001, he served as the assistant to the pastor of Mount Hermon Baptist Church in Richmond, Virginia. In 2004 and 2005, he served as the assistant to the pastor of Rising Zion Baptist Church in Cumberland, Virginia. From 2007 to 2009, he served as the superintendent of Sunday school at First Shiloh Baptist Church of Mechanicsville, Virginia. In January 2010, he accepted the position of assistant and youth pastor of Springfield Baptist Church of Mechanicsville, Virginia. In April 2013, he was called to pastor the Greenbrier Baptist Church of Arlington, Virginia, and served there for four years. In 2020, he started LivingGrace Ministries.

Dandridge has a great sense of humor. He loves to read and travel. He loves being a family man and is passionate about making the world a better place.

AMERICA, THE BEAUTIFUL NARCISSIST
TeLisa Daughtry

Being Black in America is much like being in love with a narcissist. Wait. I'll explain.

We initially fall in love with all the beautiful qualities we see, the beautiful lies we are told, the dreams we are sold, and the visions and hopes of what our love could grow to be. But, we just can't seem to ever get, or stay, on the same page, because lies, pride, manipulation, gas-lighting, and ego always seem to be in the way. This is *America*.

The foundation on which any relationship is built determines how secure the partnership will be. So, therefore, if the foundation of this nation was built on violence, lies, hate, manipulation, and thievery, why do we expect a positive and fruitful union?

The truth is … America's relationship with Black people was inevitably doomed from the start—from its first slaughters of indigenous copper peoples on these lands and the content of Africa to its first captives, its fleet of slave ships, and offering up slaves for sale. America has never loved us, never valued us, never respected us, and has never given us truth, justice, equality, or freedom.

149

One day, we woke up and said, "F*** this. F*** you! I'm done, *done!*" Then America was like, "Wait, whoa, whoa. Why are you so angry, Black people?"

Well, perhaps it's because you abuse us, you belittle us, you devalue us, you dishonor us, you lie to us, you steal from us, you oppress us, *and you kill us.* You *kill our children,* and you *kill our mothers and fathers,* and *you kill our leaders,* and you *kill us again* in the media after you have *killed us.* Then you repeat all this without any regret, regard, remorse, or reckoning for your actions. Then you say that we're making it all up, we're crazy and angry without any cause or reason, and somehow we're seeing things all wrong? But you don't see or don't seem to care. You can't seem to acknowledge *all the wrong that you continually do to us!*

Dear America, you are a *narcissist!*

How many times must we go through these toxic cycles of forgiving America and America's forgetfulness of these atrocities committed against us while our pleading, pain, and tears are constantly and repeatedly ignored? We continue to hope and do the work for change, but America has never committed to doing its part on the work needed to sustain change and heal our relationship with each other.

As a Black woman, I can attest to the *exhaustion* and *frustration* that we collectively as Black people feel, carrying the burden of always having to heal and fix things that we did not break, while we are also trying to heal and fix ourselves and deal with the ramifications of these great injustices inflicted by America on our communities. This is what it's like to be Black in America.

What needs to change, and why is it so important for change to happen sooner than later?

In order for us to achieve a real, impactful, and sustainable change—and for Black people and America to heal and transform our relationship with each other—I believe there are two things that must happen.

First and foremost, the acknowledgment of all atrocities, injustices, oppressive actions committed against, and systems designed against Black people over these past more than four hundred years. Without such acknowledgment, truth, apology, and the discussion of these things, we will never be able to truly heal as a people and as a society, and, perhaps more important, evolve from these cycles of trauma.

Second, America must commit to doing ongoing work with Black people to create actions and values that ensure an equitable future. There should be no more decisions made about Black people, nor any other groups of people, without these people in the room, at the table, and in the decision-making process. This will ensure that America is held accountable and is committed to doing the work needed.

If we are not able to achieve these two things, I sincerely fear for our collective future and for our society.

How can we learn more?

As a Black woman, there has never been a day of my existence on this earth that I have not been reminded of my race, that I have not experienced or witnessed some kind of racial injustice. That said, it is truly *exhausting* to also have to constantly educate non-Black people on why this racial injustice is a *real* problem.

In addition to the great work that the Black Lives Matter movement is doing, along with cinematic pieces like *13th*, *I Am Not Your Negro, Time: The Kalief Browder Story*, there are other great resources, accounts, and voices to follow to further educate yourself, including Jane Elliott's "Blue Eyes/Brown Eyes Exercise" with her class of third grade students in 1968. This experiment highlights "othering," and tactics used to justify discrimination and create inequalities. Sadly, Elliott's "Blue Eyes/Brown Eyes Exercise" lesson is *still* relevant. It's a tough lesson, even more than fifty years later. I strongly suggest watching the outcome from her third-grade class as adults in A *Class Divided* produced by PBS Frontline in 1985.

Books
The New Jim Crow: Mass Incarceration in the Age of Colorblindness by Michelle
    Alexander
White Fragility: Why It's So Hard for White People to Talk about Racism by Robin
        DiAngelo
An ABC of Equality by Chana Ginelle Ewing

Podcasts
"1619," *New York Times*
"Dismantling Oppression" *Checkbox Other,* NikkiInnocent.com

Social Media
BLD PWR (Build Power) engages with athletes and entertainers to use their platforms to advance radical social change and dismantle systemic oppression, bldpwr.com.

Biography

TeLisa Daughtry is an award-winning science, technology, engineering, arts, and mathematics (STEAM) diversity advocate, serial social entrepreneur, impact investor, international keynote speaker, author, multidisciplined creative technologist, and disruptor! She is the founder and chief technology officer (CTO) at FlyTechnista and impact investor at FemX Ventures. As an entrepreneur, mentor, and advocate; she is passionate about creating solutions to empower women, youth, and underrepresented groups to participate in technology and entrepreneurship. She has built several technology solutions and developed initiatives and policies supported by the United Nations Sustainable Development Goals, WeEmpower / UN Women, the President's Computer Science for All initiative in 2016, which have engaged thousands of women and girls.

Daughtry has been recognized and awarded by numerous government agencies, institutions, community organizations, and media publications for her work, achievements, and advocacy in STEAM education, technology, and diversity. As a diversity, inclusion, and equity champion, she is passionate about building diverse teams and creating inclusive environments. She has developed diversity, equity, and inclusion (DEI) strategies for more than two hundred enterprises. Additionally, as an Ariane de Rothschild Fellow, she has completed studies and training in cross-cultural leadership and innovative entrepreneurship with a focus on bridging the gap between Islamic, Jewish, and African American communities.

As an international keynote speaker with the US Department of State Bureau of Educational and Cultural Affairs, Daughtry uses her voice and visibility to educate, advocate, and elevate important and relevant topics. She has frequently spoken at the White House, the United Nations, G7 Summits, and various conferences and events.

WE ARE REPEATEDLY UNDER ASSAULT
Alana M. Hill

I have found that being Black in America means working extra hard to prove yourself . . . every day. In my experience, there is a lower perception of Black people, a diminished view of our worth and capabilities, and this is rooted in our nation's history. To own, sell, and breed people, they have to be viewed as less than; it's the only way chattel-based slavery could have existed and persisted. Less than human, less than intelligent, less than equal.

As freedom was granted, equal access to wealth and education was not. Over generations, this has translated into inequities that still exist in many systems today. To battle that, we work and teach our children that we have to be ten times as qualified as our white counterparts to succeed. This pressure has consequences on the physical, emotional, and psychological health of Black people in America.

There is a burden that we carry as Black professionals. A burden to not sully our own reputations or that of our entire race. Every mistake or misstep is credited to our collective, making the pressure to excel a constant in our lives. This pressure comes not only from our white peers (and teachers) but also from those within our community as a means to ensure that we don't ruin it for the next one.

When it comes to racial justice, it's hard to escape the stigma of being criminalized just for doing everyday things. As a Texan, the death of twenty-eight-year-old Sandra Bland affected me deeply. To feel that an encounter with an officer (over a turn signal) could lead to the kind of physical abuse she endured is deeply upsetting.

We're told to be polite and it won't happen to us, but in scene after scene, I see women who look like me, or men who look like my sons, brutalized at the blink of an eye. We give our teen boys "the talk" in hopes that they will follow Jim Crow-like mannerisms and submit fully to any indignities by police or angry citizens thrown their way just to stay alive.

These assaults on our bodies and minds are not new. I was an active college student when Rodney King was brutally beaten in Los Angeles in 1991. I thought, "*Surely, they'll see the tape and find them guilty.*" That wasn't the case then, and, almost thirty years later, it's still too often not the case. Regardless of our education, work ethic, or any other excuse that is used to mischaracterize Black lives, we are repeatedly under assault.

What needs to change, and why is it so important for change to happen sooner than later?

The change that we need to see is in equal and affirmative access to opportunities in education and the workplace. The disparity in representation of Black people in America in numerous fields, especially science, technology, engineering, and math (STEM) fields is blaring. And because these fields account for the majority of high-paying jobs, we see why the wealth and opportunity gap is far from being addressed. This essential change will create generational wealth and will create equity in America. It will also address the downward trend of prosperity that the Black community has been facing, as we are stereotyped and denied opportunities.

In addition, we need swift reform of policing practices and policies that too often threaten the physical and emotional well-being of Black citizens. There is evidence that officers are trained to de-escalate, we've seen it work with white suspects. What is missing are the consequences and sanctions of such actions to drive consistent behavior.

How can we learn more?

Anti-Black racism is infused into the foundation of our nation. The early chief architects of our nation and its founding principles established systems that were to the detriment of Black Americans. To understand this historical context and the actions to work toward dismantling racial injustice, I recommend *The Color of Compromise: The Truth about the American Church's Complicity in Racism* by Jemar Tisby. It is a book and also a documentary series that covers the cultural, political, and moral evolution of racism in America and how to combat it. To have true reconciliation, the house needs to be renovated while the foundation is repaired.

Postscript: An Important Letter

Dear White Christians,

I love you, and God loves you; but He needs you to understand some things. I need you to understand some things:

1. It is not (insert the name of a Black person you know)'s responsibility to educate you on the history of our country and White supremacy's role in its founding. It is well-documented. Please read or watch *The Color of Compromise*.

When you say this country was founded as a Christian nation, you leave out its formation of racist systems and how it codified oppression and treated the Natives and enslaved Africans as beasts to be slain or tamed.

2. If you want racial "reconciliation," you have to be willing to go back to 1619 to when we first met. No, it wasn't you, and it wasn't me; but it was our races. As my husband, Rodney, once so eloquently stated, Black people are still very connected to our ancestors. "We" were in the bowels of those ships. Our relationship (that you want to restore) was NEVER right, so we're not getting back together. We need to re-establish together.

3. Whether you were rich or poor, you have White privilege. Stop arguing about it, stop resisting it, and START using it as a kingdom tool. You are in spaces we are not. Speak for the people you say you love. If you need help with that, then read *Be the Bridge: Pursuing God's Heart for Racial Reconciliation.*

4. Service AND Solidarity—don't pick one; live both. Don't feed poor Black children and pity them; work to dismantle the systems that have them living like that. When a Black brother or sister is slain on video, don't search the Internet for his/her traffic tickets or other misdeeds. Call wrong "wrong." Flip over some tables. Use your power and privilege.

Purpose is about realizing who you uniquely are and knowing WHY you are. It's using your strengths, your position, and your voice for the kingdom and the world. Battling racism, injustice, inequity, and oppression should be part of that. The next time you donate to a charity, ask yourself WHY that charity needs to exist. Pray and ask God what you can/should do with that revelation. Remember, faith without works is DEAD!

Sincerely,
Your Black Christian Sister

Biography

Alana M. Hill, project management professional (PMP), is a resilient, compassionate, and eager professional, wife, and mother. She has committed her life to serving others, and she does so through speaking, writing, and leading change. Hill has a Bachelor of Science in engineering degree from Texas A&M University, which deeply informed her advocacy for racial equity in STEM. Her inner-city background remains a lens through which she views justice and opportunity. As the only woman of color in many spaces, Hill is painfully aware of the consequences of microaggressions and blatant racism in the workplace. In addition, she is the mom of four Black sons, whose lives and hearts she's worked tirelessly to protect.

Hill's consultancy leverages her expertise as an international change leader, helping people lead change in their lives and their organizations. She is dedicated to building resilient change leaders with a critical eye and a compassionate spirit. With over twenty years of cross-functional leadership and training expertise, Hill helps individuals and organizations accomplish their goals by utilizing sharp analysis, strategic planning, and interpersonal skills development.

Hill is the author of three books. The latest, *What's Your Catalyst? The Power of Managed Change,* guides readers to discover their purpose, passions, and priorities to become more effective change leaders at work and at home. When she is not traveling the globe, Hill can be found running and serving in her church and community.

BEING BLACK IS BOTH A BLESSING AND A CURSE
Paul Johnson

I was born in New Orleans, however, my family moved away when I was a young boy. My parents shared that one of the primary reasons our family left Louisiana was because they had concerns about the safety of my three brothers and me. They believed that moving to Washington state would reduce the odds of their four sons getting entangled in a criminal justice system that has historically been stacked against African American males, particularly in places like Louisiana.

Growing up in Seattle was far from perfect, and this part of the country was no utopia. Being far away from my extended family presented trade-offs, but being in Seattle likely provided a buffer from some challenges I saw friends and family experiencing in the South. I have learned that being Black anywhere in America comes with a set of additional burdens.

I love the fact that I am a Black man. There are times when I feel that being Black in America is both a blessing and a curse. I consider it a blessing to be Black because it comes with a rich history and legacy of greatness. I frequently think about role models who came before me—individuals like Thurgood Marshall, Fannie Lou Hamer, Jackie Robinson, Ida B. Wells, and so many others.

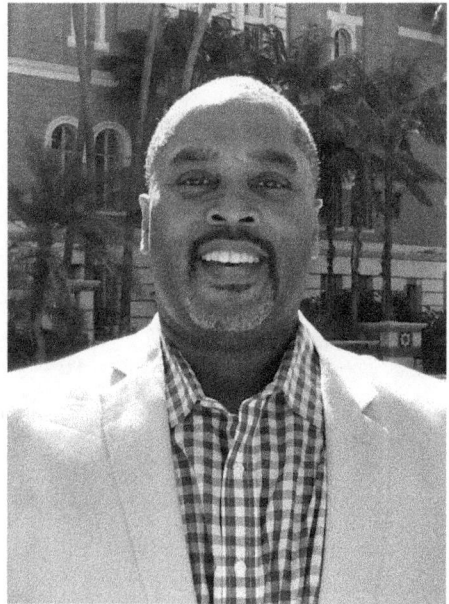

I remember being in fifth grade and giving a presentation in school about Benjamin Banneker to my mostly non-Black classmates. I recall feeling a sense of great pride as I spoke about the brilliance of a Black man. Born a son of slaves, he achieved a level of greatness as an early architect and city designer of our nation's capital, despite operating on an uneven playing field.

Decades since giving that school report, I find myself filled with pride and joy each time I hear a great artist like Stevie Wonder, Wynton Marsalis, or Jill Scott or when I watch Denzel Washington, Viola Davis, or Will Smith in a feature film. What gives me the greatest joy is when I witness proud Black Americans fighting for justice and equity.

The image of John Carlos and Tommie Smith with raised fists, donning a single black glove at the 1968 Olympics in Mexico City is forever burned into my memory. It is a peculiar memory to have because I was only a two-year-old baby in 1968 and did not likely see the event that October, but I have always felt like I was there with them in spirit. I felt a similar sense of pride when I witnessed Colin Kaepernick taking a knee before his National Football League (NFL) games in 2017 to protest against police brutality.

It inspires me to see individuals who look like me, who are willing to sacrifice a certain degree of comfort, and risk personal rewards to speak out against racism and oppression.

The blessing of being Black begins to feel more like a curse when racism rears its head and blackness becomes a target for discrimination, hatred, and violence. I was angered, like most Americans, by the video of George Floyd being murdered by officers in Minneapolis, but I was equally disturbed by the killings of Eric Garner, Charleena Lyles; Walter Scott; Philando Castile; Korryn Gaines; Michael Brown, Jr.; Miriam Carey; Manuel Ellis; Terence Crutcher; Elijah McClain; and so many others that were captured on video.

It angers me that so many Black men and women are brutalized and killed by officers of the law—people who are hired as public servants and paid with taxpayer dollars to protect the people in the communities they serve. The negligence and disregard make me think about other Black citizens like Sandra Bland; Freddie Carlos Gray, Jr.; and individuals who died during encounters with police officers but where there had not been video evidence to confirm that they were murdered. It hurts my heart that we will probably never know the full story behind many cases where Black citizens never made it home safely to their families.

I also fear that seeing multiple videos of Black bodies being brutalized will eventually enable viewers to become more and more desensitized to the violence against Black bodies. I fear that there are hundreds of similar incidents that are never captured on film. History tells us that we are unable to trust the testimony or version of events shared by authorities and members of the criminal justice system. There is a serious lack of accountability and a need for full-scale reform in our criminal justice system.

Atatiana Jefferson, Botham Jean, and Breonna Taylor were all in the sanctuary of their homes, likely feeling a high degree of safety and secureness. All three were killed by police officers in unprovoked attacks, and we continue to see police brutality and a lack of accountability. Only two weeks after the murder of George Floyd, we witnessed the senseless murder of Rayshard Brooks in an Atlanta fast-food parking lot.

Perhaps the case that upset me the most was the murder of Tamir Rice. He was a twelve-year-old child who had so many years of life ahead of him. Sadly, his family will never see Tamir become a father, a grandfather, an uncle, etcetera. Tamir will never have an opportunity to walk across a stage at graduation, or walk a daughter down the aisle at her wedding, or teach his son how to ride a bike. It also hurt because he was simply playing with a toy gun in a park when an officer killed him in cold blood—just a small child, playing on a playground in the manner that I played many times as a child.

Two cases that didn't involve police officers but that bothered me just as much were the killings of Ahmaud Arbery and Trayvon Martin. These killings were carried out by vigilantes without badges. The killers were simply rogue citizens who felt it was within their constitutional rights and their duty to take matters into their own hands and act as judge, jury, and executioner.

It is important that we teach our children about various unwritten rules when they are engaging with members of law enforcement. Keep your hands where they can see them; never run away; do not reach for your wallet, phone, etcetera. We teach them while understanding that these rules do not always guarantee the safety of our children, but the teachings might increase the odds of them coming home alive. There is a proverbial playbook for coaching our children on how to engage with members of law enforcement, but there is no playbook for dealing with self-deputized militias or bullies with guns. How do we prepare our children to deal with those who decide to take up arms and hunt them? I don't have all the answers, but I plan to do whatever I can to change the narrative.

What needs to change, and why is it so important for change to happen sooner than later?

Greater police accountability is incredibly important. This is a change that can happen sooner than later and that really needs to happen as soon as possible. The brutality and abuse of power has persisted far too long. It is perplexing and frustrating at the same time because I hear people asking questions like "How did we get here?"

This is an interesting question because more than fifty years ago, US President Lyndon B. Johnson formed the National Advisory Commission on Civil Disorders to do research to better understand America's race problem. However, instead of applying a concerted effort to mitigate the issues revealed in the commission's Kerner Report, the research was largely ignored by US leadership and administrations. The country has had five decades to tackle this problem, but the equity and wealth gap between African Americans and their white counterparts has only widened.

> Many Americans blamed the riots on outside agitators or young black men, who represented the largest and most visible group of rioters. But, in March 1968, the Kerner Commission turned those assumptions upside-down, declaring white racism—not black anger—turned the key that unlocked urban American turmoil.
>
> Bad policing practices, a flawed justice system, unscrupulous consumer credit practices, poor or inadequate housing, high unemployment, voter suppression, and other culturally embedded forms of racial discrimination all converged to propel violent upheaval on the streets of African-American neighborhoods in American cities, north and south, east and west. And as black unrest arose, inadequately trained police officers and National Guard troops entered affected neighborhoods, often worsening the violence.

—Alice George
"The 1968 Kerner Commission Got It Right, But Nobody Listened,"
Smithsonian Magazine
March 1, 2018

As a result of ignoring the Kerner Commission, the country is still suffering from willful ignorance, and Americans continue asking the same rhetorical questions in 2020. Coming up with answers will not matter if the country continues to ignore the solutions.

I have always been an advocate for inclusion, equity, and issues involving social justice, but becoming a father has made these issues an absolute obsession for me. I want my son to grow up in a world where his race will not hold him back, where it will not get him profiled, where it will not put a target on his back or get him killed. Watching Black men and women abused, brutalized, and killed has become a regular segment on the daily news. Kicking the can down the road for someone else to fix this has occurred for far too long. The time is now to fix the problem.

How can we learn more?

I don't believe we can overnight solve the racial disparity problems we see in America. It took multiple centuries for America to end up here, and it will take time to repair much of the damage. However, I believe we can make gradual progress year after year if we begin having more meaningful dialogue and establishing policies that demand greater fairness and accountability from our criminal justice system.

We need to demand that our police officers have just as much formal education as we expect our schoolteachers to have. To guard against potential blind spots, police need to understand their implicit and affinity biases. Several laws and policies that currently protect police officers from accountability need to be changed. If officers break the law or abuse their power, they need to be held accountable.

The book *White Fragility: Why It's So Hard for White People to Talk about Racism* by Robin DiAngelo should be converted into a curriculum and taught to all government employees and anyone paid by taxpayer dollars. Schools in America need to incorporate mandatory lessons about the Thirteenth Amendment, the 1921 Tulsa Race Massacre, as well as facts from *The New York Times*'s The 1619 Project and how slave labor made America into the global power it has become.

Students attending schools need to better understand how money generated through the institution of slavery provided underwriting for several universities to operate and was used to provide financial support to kickstart other US industries such as manufacturing, aerospace, and agriculture. Without slavery and profits from the sugar and cotton industries, big name companies that are responsible for the cars we drive to the household and personal products we use to the beverages we drink might not have ever existed.

Biography

Paul Johnson was born in New Orleans, Louisiana. However, when he was three, his family moved to Seattle, Washington where he currently lives with his wife, Ricole, and their eight-year-old son, Roman.

Johnson has worked for several large companies in the Seattle area, mostly as a human resource professional. He regards his number one job as being a dad, a role he takes seriously. He is also passionate about learning, teaching, and leading by example. As a lifelong learner, he has never stopped attending school. After attending Seattle University for undergraduate school, he acquired graduate degrees from the University of Washington, Villanova University, and Georgetown University. He is currently in a doctorate program at the University of Southern California and hopes to teach someday. His wife is also currently in school working toward a doctoral degree in engineering. He and his wife value education and strive to serve as role models for their son and others.

Johnson was attracted to this project, *A Collective Breath*, for several reasons. He hopes to contribute, engage, and inspire others. He also resonates with the significance surrounding the date of August 28. The delivery of Dr. Martin Luther King, Jr.'s "I Have a Dream" speech, Barack Obama's acceptance of the Democratic National Convention presidential nomination, along with the birth of his son are all historic events that occurred on August 28.

CAN *YOU* BREATHE?

Clinton Harris

The year is 1991 and the Chicago Bulls are battling the Los Angeles Lakers in game five of the National Basketball Association (NBA) Finals. The Bulls led the Lakers three games to one, and their first NBA championship is within their grasp. The Bulls are not home in Chicago, they are playing in the Great Western Forum in Inglewood, California. The game is tight through every quarter, and the Bulls' stars, Michael Jordan and Scottie Pippen, are dominating Magic Johnson and the Lakers by the fourth quarter. As the final seconds tick away, the Chicago Bulls are crowned world champions for the first time in its twenty-five-year history.

A young Black boy leaves the house of his friend, one block from his home, and starts to run home as the celebrations outside begin. The boy is quite an athlete and happens to be fast and enjoys running, so he speeds up and is in a full sprint by mid-block. At thirteen years old, he is still faster than most grown men. As the boy rounds the corner to the street he lives on, he is tackled full force and slammed to the ground.

Guns are pulled and placed against his back and his skull, then he is rolled onto his stomach and handcuffed. The boy is afraid, frantic, and still out of breath from being tackled, slammed to the ground, and piled on top of. "What did I do?" the boy asks.

"Shut up before I blow your head off! You move and I'll blow your head off!" one of the officers states. The boy is afraid and confused. The neighbors come outside as they hear the ruckus, disapproving of the tactics used and especially the tactics being used against this particular boy.

A second police unit arrives, and the officers snatch the boy off the ground and force him into the police car as if he were a rag doll. The boy is now being transported by the two officers who initially tackled him and threatened his life. He is alone and scared for what is to come. This boy—who had no criminal record, had never been arrested, was a good student, was considered extremely respectful to all those in the neighborhood—was now in handcuffs bloodied and bruised from his ordeal, being transported to the police station. He still didn't even have a clue why.

A busted lip, a knot on his head, scrapes and scratches all over him, and absolute fear permeating him, this boy was handcuffed to a wall in a concrete room. Three hours later, the door opens, and the same two officers enter the room and uncuff the young boy. They take him to their car and drop him off where the ordeal began. These two Caucasian officers offered a simple, "We thought you were someone else" as their apology and drove away, leaving the boy where they'd picked him up and beat him up, both externally and mentally on that summer day.

Can you imagine what that boy felt like? What fear he had for police for a time after that ordeal? Would you like to ask him? Then ask me . . . because that boy was me.

That's what it's like to be Black in America.

What needs to change, and why is it so important for change to happen sooner than later?

There are myriad things that need to change in this nation, sooner rather than later. Foremost, the ideology and mindset of individuals in this nation needs to change. Let's begin with the ideologies that have created the mindset of racial inequality. First, we cannot begin to have a mindset without being bombarded by an idea. In this case, that idea leads to hate, subjugation, segregation, murder, and bigotry. This is where change has to begin and end, not only by those who believe these ideas, but it has to be extinguished before those ideas can be bequeathed to the next generation. This is where we must take the first steps of the process that lead toward the final steps of a long journey.

A glaring example of why we need to eradicate these ideologies can be found in the innocence of a child. Children can be placed in a preschool among toys and not one of them will care whether the child next to them is Black, White, Asian, Hispanic, Native, Pacific Islander, or any other race, religion, or creed. Sadly, once we place those same children in a room together just a few years later, perhaps even later in grade school or middle school, those same children now recognize the racial differences between them and see that as a reason for some form of segregation or racial hierarchy.

These ideas are programmed and implanted at an early age, either via the society these children are within and/or the family these children are raised within. This is not to say that all children will have negative thoughts toward a race not of their own; it just lends to the idea that society has allowed negative racial ideologies to flourish to a point where it poisons the minds and thoughts of those of subsequent generations, if it's allowed and encouraged.

Seeing that this nation is now facing its greatest racial strain since the murder of Dr. Martin Luther King, Jr., it is evident that nothing has stopped the seepage of negative racial ideologies. With current President Donald Trump, those negative ideologies will only be perpetuated and exacerbated. This is not based on political party lines, this is based on right and wrong, and has implications for life and death.

As stated, change needs to come in the form of all individuals moving beyond the ignorance of acceptance and tolerance for that which they could not, and would not, tolerate themselves. Change must come from those who chose to remain silent in the face of that which does not directly affect them. Change must come in the election of leaders on the local, state, and federal levels that will create positive change for the masses, not stagnant existence for privileged.

We can no longer allow those who seek to subjugate entire groups of people to lead this nation. To be perfectly blunt, we can no longer allow anyone to overlook and intentionally crush the civil liberties of anyone, simply because they are different The question here is, "What are you, the reader, willing to permanently change within yourself and your actions to allow everyone the right to exist? How many more people will it take to say, "I can't breathe," before you take notice and make individual action for change?

> It may well be that we will have to repent in this generation, not merely for the vitriolic words and the violent actions of the bad people . . . but for the appalling silence and indifference of the good people who sit around and say wait on time.

> —Dr. Martin Luther King, Jr.
> Speech at Illinois Wesleyan University
> February 10, 1966

Can *you* breathe?

How can we learn more?

The 2012 PBS documentary, *Slavery by Another Name: The Re-Enslavement of Black Americans from the Civil War to World War II* directed by Sam Pollard and based on the book by Douglas A. Blackmon, challenges the thought that slavery truly ended with the statements and legislation put forth after the Emancipation Proclamation in 1863. For sixty years after the Emancipation Proclamation, Caucasian individuals found a means to slip past and bend the laws based on common tolerance. Black men and women were brutally forced back into labor, often being accused of crimes they didn't commit to do so.

This documentary resonated with me and should be watched, as even in today's world, laws are bent due to common tolerances to fit the ideologies of some Caucasians with the old-school racial ignorance and mindset toward the Black race. Keeping in mind that this is still an issue, we can see that these individuals will do whatever they can to keep their perceived racial superiority status intact, as opposed to accepting that all people are created equal.

Biography

Clinton Harris is a personal development expert, life progression coach, entrepreneur, keynote motivational speaker, and number one best-selling author. He has worked with many well-respected experts in his field. Working in organizational leadership, educational institutions, with families and the military, he has served to help people all over the world for more than a decade.

RESOURCES FOR ADDITIONAL LEARNING

Books, Articles, and Additional Readings

Sarah Shakour and Madeleine Hillyer, "4 Ways to be an Ally in the Fight Against Racism, *World Economic Forum*, June 19, 2020.

Dion Rabouin, "10 Myths About the Racial Wealth Gap," *Axios*, July 23, 2020.

The 1619 Project, essays, *The New York Times Magazine*, 2019.

An ABC of Equality, Chana Ginelle Ewing, 2019.

Meghan Rabbit, The Alzheimer's Epidemic No One is Talking About," *The O Magazine*, July/August 2020.

James John and Margaret Goff, "Anti-Black Racism: Where We Were, and Where We Are Today," *Urban Institute*, August 14, 2016.

Automating Inequality: How High-Tech Tools Profile, Police and Punish the Poor, Virginia Eubanks, 2019.

Katie Barnes, "Barnes: LeBron James and Nneka Ogwumike didn't teach me that racism is a problem in this country," *ESPN*, August 27, 2020.

Between the World and Me, Ta-Nehisi Coates, 2015.

Black Americans, Alphonso Pinkney, 1999.

A Black Women's History of the United States, Daina Ramey Berry and Kali Nicole Gross, 2020.

Black Wealth/White Wealth: A New Perspective on Racial Inequality, Melvin Oliver and Thomas Shapiro, 2006.

Books, Articles, and Additional Readings cont.

Blackballed: The Black Vote and U.S. Democracy, Darryl Pinckney, 2014.

Blue Eyes/Brown Eyes Exercise, Jane Elliott, 1968.

Caste: The Origins of Our Discontent. Isabel Wilkerson, 2020.

Chains and Images of Psychological Slavery, Na'im Akbar, 1984.

The Color of Compromise: The Truth about the American Church's Complicity in Racism, Jemar Tisby, 2019.

The Color of Law: A Forgotten History of How Our Government Segregated America, Richard Rothstein, 2018.

The Color of Money: Black Banks and the Racial Wealth Gap, Mehrsa Baradaran, 2019.

Code of the Street: Decency Violence, and the Moral Life of the Inner City, Elijah Anderson, 2000.

Maja Hazell, "The Crippling Impact of Anti-Black Racism, and How Allies Can Act Against It." *Law.com,* June 18, 2020.

Dog Whistle Politics: How Coded Racial Appeals Have Reinvented Racism and Wrecked the Middle Class, Ian Hanley López, 2015.

The Ethnic Project: Transforming Racial Fiction into Ethnic Factions, Vilna Bashi Treitler, 2013.

For Jobs and Freedom: Race and Labor in America Since 1865, Robert H. Zieger, 2010.

From the War on Poverty to the War on Crime: The Making of Mass Incarceration in America, Elizabeth Hinton, 2017

Books, Articles, and Additional Readings cont.

The Hollywood Jim Crow: The Racial Politics of the Movie Industry, Maryann Erigha, 2019.

How to Be an Antiracist, Ibram X. Kendi, 2019.

How to be Less Stupid About Race, Crystal M. Fleming, 2019.

Alejandra Borunda, "How 'Nature Deprived' Neighborhoods Impact the Health of People of Color, *National Geographic*, July 29, 2020.

Improving Your Serve: The Art of Unselfish Living, Charles R. Swindoll, 1981.

Jill Lepore, "The Invention of the Police," *The New Yorker*, July 13, 2020.

Just Mercy: A Story of Justice and Redemption, Bryan Stevenson, 2015.

Letter from Birmingham Jail, Martin Luther King, Jr., 1963.

Me and White Supremacy: Combat Racism, Change the World, and Become a Good Ancestor, Layla F. Saad, 2020.

Medical Apartheid: The Dark History of Medical Experimentation on Black Americans from Colonial Times to the Present, Harriet Washington, 2008.

Medical Bondage: Race, Gender, and the Origins of American Gynecology, Deirdre Cooper Owens, 2018.

The Mis-Education of the Negro, Carter G. Woodson, 1933.

Narrative of the Life of Frederick Douglass, an American Slave, Frederick Douglass, 1845.

The New Jim Crow: Mass Incarceration in the Age of Colorblindness, Michelle Alexander, 2020.

Books, Articles, and Additional Readings cont.

The Origin of Others, Toni Morrison, 2017. *2019.*

Race and Racisms: A Critical Approach, Tanya Maria Golash-Boza, 2017.

Race for Profit: How Banks and the Real Estate Industry Undermined Black Homeownership, Keeanga-Yamahtta Taylor, 2019.

Racism Without Racists: Color-Blind Racism and the Persistence of Racial Inequality in America, Eduardo Bonilla-Silva, 2017.

Racist America: Roots, Current Realities, and Future Reparations, Joe R. Feagin, 2018.

Roots: The Saga of An American Family, Alex Haley, 1974.

Slavery by Another Name: The Re-Enslavement of Black Americans from the Civil War to World War II, documentary, director Sam Pollard, 2012.

Slavery by Another Name: The Re-Enslavement of Black Americans from the Civil War to World War II, Douglas A. Blackmon, 2009.

So You Want to Talk About Race, Ieoma Oluo, 2019.

Stamped: Racism, Antiracism, and You, Jason Reynolds and Ibram X. Kendi, 2020.

Stamped from the Beginning: The Definitive History of Racist Ideas in America, Ibram X. Kendi, 2017.

The Souls of Black Folk, W.E.B Du Bois, 1903.

A Terrible Thing to Waste: Environmental Racism and Its Assault on the American Mind, Harriet A. Washington, 2020.

Elizabeth Alexander, "The Travon Generation," *The New Yorker,* June 15, 2020.

Thick: And Other Essays, Tressie McMillian Cottom, 2019.

Books, Articles, and Additional Readings cont.

Time: The Kalief Browder Story, documentary, director Jenner Furst, 2017.

Two-Faced Racism: Whites in the Backstage and Frontstage, Leslie Houts Picca and Joe R. Feagin, 2007.

Uncle Tom's Cabin, Harriet Beecher Stowe, 1852.

Nikita Stewart, "We Are Committing Educational Malpractice: Why Slavery is Mistaught—and Worse—in American Schools," *The New York Times Magazine,* August 19, 2019.

Anne Helen Petersen, "What Happened in Bethel, Ohio?" *BuzzFeed,* July 5, 2020.

White Fragility: Why It's So Hard for White People to Talk about Racism, Robin DiAngelo, 2018.

White Like Me: Reflections on Race from a Privileged Son, Tim Wise, 2011.

White Privilege: Essential Readings on the Other Side of Racism, 5e, Paula S. Rothenberg, 2016.

White Rage: The Unspoken Truth of Our Racial Divide, Carol Anderson, 2016.

Why Black People Tend to Shout: Cold Facts and Wry Views from a Black Man's World, Ralph Wiley, 1991.

Why Are All the Black Kids Sitting Together in the Cafeteria?: And Other Conversations About Race, Beverly Daniel Tatum, 2017.

Why We Can't Wait, Martin Luther King, Jr., 1963.

The Wretched of the Earth, Frantz Fanon, 2005.

Documentaries, Episodes Miniseries, TV Series, and Videos

13th, documentary, director Ava DuVernay, 2016.

Black America Since MLK: And Still I Rise, PBS series, director Leslie Asako Gladsjo, 2016.

A Class Divided, documentary, director William Peters, PBS Frontline, 1985.

The Color of Compromise Video Study, twelve episodes, starring Jemar Tisby, 2020.

Hidden Colors: The Untold History of People of Aboriginal, Moor, and African Descent, documentary, director Tariq Nasheed, 2011.

I Am Not Your Negro, documentary, director Raoul Peck, 2017.

JusticeCon, conference video, https://www.youtube.com/watch?v=k3qjGl_DEuE.

LA 92, documentary, directors Daniel Lindsay and T. J. Martin, 2017.

MILWAUKEE 53206, documentary, director Keith McQuirter, 2016.

Teach Us All, documentary, director Sonia Lowman, 2017.

When They See Us, TV miniseries, writer and director Ava DuVernay, 2019.

Whose Streets? documentary, directors Sabaah Folayan and Damon Davis, 2017.

Podcasts

1619, *New York Times,* 2019.

Dismantling Oppression, *Checkbox Other,* NikkiInnocent.com.

Floodlines, *The Atlantic,* 2020.

Podcasts cont.

Inclusion School, 2020

Intersectionality Matters! 2018.

Silence is Not an Option, *CNN*, 2020.

Throughline, *NPR*, 2019.

Uncomfortable Conversations With a Black Man, 2020.

Websites

Anti-Racism Resources List, https://bit.ly/2NHhqk6.

BLD PWR (Build Power), bldpwr.com.

D. L. Hughley, http://realdlhughley.com/.

The Emmett Till Legacy Foundation, https://emmetttilllegacyfoundation.com

Equal Justice Initiative, https://eji.org/.

Grassroots Law Project, https://www.grassrootslaw.org/.

LiveFreeUSA, http://www.livefreeusa.org/.

The AND Campaign, https://andcampaign.org/.

About the Compiler

BRIDGETT McGOWEN-HAWKINS

"Talks too much" was a comment Bridgett consistently received on her elementary school report cards. Early on, she developed a love for speaking, words, and books—so much so until she was always the first to volunteer to read passages aloud in class, and during moments of boredom in her third- and fourth-grade classes, she would analyze the dictionary, jotting down those words and definitions she found particularly interesting.

With reading as a favorite pastime and little to no fear of speaking in front of a crowd, it only makes sense that Bridgett is now an award-winning international professional speaker and the CEO of BMcTALKS Press, an independent publishing company where she thrives in an environment that positions her to bring other people's words to life. Bridgett's résumé also includes being a 2019-2020 member of Forbes Coaches Council and launching BMcTALKS Academy where, as the founder and owner, she offers online self-paced courses to move professionals to use their voices to monetize their expertise.

Since 2001, Bridgett has been a professional speaker, and she has appeared on programs alongside several prominent figures such as former President Barack Obama, Deepak Chopra, Alex Rodriguez (A-Rod), Oprah Winfrey, Shonda Rhimes, Katie Couric, Chip Gaines, and Janelle Monáe.

The prestigious University of Texas at Austin presented her with a Master Presenter Award in 2006; Canada-based One Woman has presented her with two Fearless Woman Awards; and she has facilitated hundreds of workshops, keynote and commencement ad-dresses, conference sessions, trainings, and webinars to thousands of students and professionals who are positioned all around the globe.

Bridgett's expertise and presentations have been sought after by companies, post-secondary institutions, and organizations such as Society for Human Resource Management (SHRM), Vanguard Investments, Norton LifeLock, Symantec, Kentucky Fried Chicken, McGraw-Hill Education, LinkedIn Local, Association for Talent Development (ATD), Doña Ana Community College, North Carolina Chamber of Commerce, National Association of Women Sales Professionals, Independence University, Arizona Private School Association, Turnitin, Texas Healthcare Trustees, National Association of Black Accountants, Greater Phoenix Convention & Visitors Bureau, and Prairie View A&M University.

Forbes, LinkedIn, and Thrive Global are a few of the platforms where you can find articles penned by Bridgett. In addition, she has been quoted by Transizion, has contributed to UpJourney, and has appeared as a guest on The Training and Learning Development Company's TLDCast, Phoenix Business Radio, and a multitude of podcasts to showcase her expertise in the professional speaking industry. Her work has been highlighted by *VoyagePhoenix Magazine*; award-winning Scottsdale-based branding and consulting agency, Catalyst; The Startup Growth; and her alma mater, Prairie View A&M University (PVAMU), the second oldest institution of higher education in the state of Texas and a part of the Texas A&M University System.

Bridgett has also taught for PVAMU, Lone Star College System, and University of Phoenix. She graduated cum laude with her bachelor's degree in communication, and one year later, she graduated summa cum laude with her master's degree. She is a Forbes contributor; a publisher; a member of Entrepreneur Leadership Network, a member of International Society of Female Professionals; a former member of National Speakers Association; and a member of Alpha Kappa Alpha Sorority, Incorporated.

In 2019, Bridgett authored and published two books, *REAL TALK: What Other Experts Won't Tell You About How to Make Presentations That Sizzle* as well as *Rise and Sizzle: Daily Communication and Presentation Strategies for Sales, Business, and Higher Ed Pros*, the former of which sold out within minutes of her presentation concluding at ATD's 76th annual international conference and exposition in Washington, D.C. and which was also a finalist for a 2020 Next Generation Indie Book Award.

In January 2020, she also wrote and published *Show Up and Show Out: 52 Communication Habits to Make You Unforgettable*, which sold out at the annual Think Better Live Better event hosted in February 2020 in San Diego, California by *New York Times* best-sellers Marc and Angel Chernoff. Days later, she published her first compilation, *Own the Microphone: How 50 of the World's Best Professional Speakers Launched Their Careers (and How You Can, Too!)* Four months later, in June 2020, her second and third compilations, *Triumph Over the Trials* and *Redesign Your 9-to-5*, were published, and her first podcast is due for a late-summer 2020 release.

Bridgett's mission is to work beyond the hours of 9am to 5pm to help scores of professionals turn their words and voices into powerhouses, inspire millions, and build serious skill sets and mindsets that will lead to more and more opportunities.

Bridgett is married to Aaron Hawkins, and he makes her laugh every day. Their family resides in the Phoenix, Arizona area. Bridgett enjoys frequent summertime getaways to San Diego, and she absolutely loves beautiful sunsets.

ABOUT BMcTALKS PRESS

BMcTALKS Press is an independent publishing company that provides a full suite of publishing services to new authors.

We design, create, and deliver high-quality trade books and eBooks that expand your brand, support your vision, and solidify you as a contender in your industry.

BMcTALKS Press knows so many are passionate about that in which they believe and the work they do. We empower aspiring authors to realize the expertise, savviness, acumen, and passion they bring to the world, and we assist you with identifying avenues for achieving the goal of becoming published authors so your words can change the world.

When you get published, you position yourself to ...
- Add "published author" to your already impressive list of accomplishments
- Establish yourself as an authority and an expert on a topic
- Have a book that serves as an "elevated business card"
- Provide added value to your clients
- Support and expand your brand
- Give your followers another way to connect with you
- Share an important message with the world
- Leave a legacy
- Grow your business
- Make an impact
- Get your message out to the world

Visit **www.bmctalkspress.com** to schedule your complimentary, no-obligation call to discuss your book idea.

Do you already have a completed manuscript?
Submit it to **info@bmtpress.com,** and let us get to work for you.

Let's print your passion!